DOG WALKING FOR BEGINNERS

Andy Gibney

First published in 2025 in the UK
3P2, Tailby House,
Bath Road, Kettering
NN16 8NL

A catalogue number for this book is available
from the British Library

ISBN: 978-1-913740-80-1

Cover design: James Mossop

For mother
Diana Jacqueline Gibney
(1938 – 2025)

Contents:

Prologue
Chasing rabbits

Owning a dog is many hours of relaxed fun, loving moments, hilarity and feeding combined with the occasional moments of heart-stopping terror. This is one of those moments.

It's August 2022; it's bright, sunny and you might imagine, idyllic. I'm in a field which centuries ago housed a Roman villa, but today is used mostly by dog walkers. With that in mind you would think, with the busy A43 on the other side of the tree line twenty metres from the field, that the fence that encloses the field would be secure and not have any holes. Unfortunately, this is not the case. The developer tells the residents that they have to allow the holes for the deer. The deer that never frequent the field and if they did, could jump the fence without missing a beat. Meanwhile, the terror.

I bring my dog to this field every day. We wander around, mostly off lead, where he mixes with other dogs and sniffs the many smells. He is almost three years old and has the energy of a three-year-old human. He is a quick dog, a cross between a Collie and a German Shepherd, and probably a lot more, and has one fatal flaw. He loves chasing other animals. Dogs, when at play. Birds, squirrels, cats (if they run) and rabbits.

Today it was rabbits.

Early in the morning the rabbits are still busy from the previous night's gaiety and often found hopping about the field. A field that possibly saw two hundred dogs a day. My concern was my dog as he hurtled towards a cotton tail disappearing through the fence. And he knew where the holes were.

I screamed his name. No response. I ran across the grass to the gate in the middle of the fence. The view which greeted me haunts me to this day. The road is a busy A road and bypasses the village of Weldon, some five miles from the town of Corby in Northamptonshire. It links a roundabout at the top end and another at the bottom end. It's about a mile in length and cars and trucks will get up to 60mph along there. But this morning, as I saw, traffic was at a standstill.

A white Mercedes was pulled across the road. Some 200m from where I stood a black Mercedes was pulled over on the left-hand side, heading up the hill and an attractive, well-dressed woman was out of her car. On the right, a truck had stopped and traffic was now lining up behind it. And my dog, my bundle of joy, the animal who was helping to keep me sane was trotting up the road towards the attractive woman. Him without a care in the world. Me wondering how this dog had managed to stay alive. Plus, of course, the shame. No one looks at a dog in this situation. They look at the owner. Me. The idiot who didn't have his dog on a lead. The lucky fool who was not scraping his dog off the tarmac. The irresponsible owner who should know better. The man who had almost caused a multi-car pileup. The man who had enough on his plate without the situation in front of him.

I thought all of this as I jogged up the road and took the animal from the lady, put him on his lead and walked him back towards the field. The black Mercedes drove off without a word of admonishment. The white Mercedes, whose owner I would later learn was a business owner I knew (let the shame envelope me), moved and cleared the road and the lorry driver drove on too. Followed by the dozen backed up cars. I disappeared into the field. I quietly told my dog off (shouting wouldn't help), counted all my blessings, of which there many and headed home. Now three years on, I don't know how I would have coped had he been killed that day. Another dog had been killed on that road around that time and that was an animal waiting on the side of the road when an out-of-control car clipped its head killing it on impact. Numerous cats and roadkill are also slaughtered on the same road. I had had a lucky escape. My dog was oblivious to all of this. Inside, the adrenalin now kicked in and I wanted to cry with relief. Instead, we walked the half mile back to our home.

Sabat, for that is his name, is my first dog. How I got him and what lead me to this point, and beyond, is revealed in these pages. As a dog owner with no clue, at the time, welcome to dog walking for beginners.

Part One

Three Hearts

Chapter 1
Romanian summer

Bucharest in July 2019 was hot and uncomfortable. Even more so if you were a dog with six pups waiting to be born. They were hidden in an alley near an industrial garbage bin, where the shade it gave helped the mother deliver her pups into a steamy morning.

Instinctively she began to lick them clean and just as instinctively the blind babies found their way to her nipples which were bursting with milk. As the pups took their first meal the tired mother panted in the rising heat.

Fortunately, that day wasn't as hot as it had been recently with temperatures in the 25C range. The day before it had been 33C and the poor mother thought she would pass out. Delivering her pups had been a blessing and now she had time to rest.

All around the sounds of the city bellowed. Car horns, screeching brakes, shouting, swearing, laughing and music coming from open windows that would have disturbed most family pets, but this little family only knew the streets. It hadn't been far from where she was now that she became pregnant sixty-three days before. She hadn't seen the father again and this first litter became her problem from day one. She had done well to get this far.

For a day or two, she lay in the shade of the huge garbage bin, trying to stay cool as the temperature rose. The pups cried in the heat and suckled when they could, but the mother knew she had to eat as well. In the city there were always scraps to eat and the garbage bin itself provided overflows from the restaurant it sat behind.

Three days after the pups were born the bin men came and she knew she had to move her little family away. Romanian bin men had a reputation for throwing street dogs straight into the back of the garbage truck, breaking the pathetic animals alive as they squealed and then snapped in half as the teeth of the crusher took their lives. This mumma wasn't having that.

She gathered the still blind pups together and herded them away from the alley when she heard the bin men approaching. She had to find somewhere with shade and six puppies weren't helping the task. Still a young female dog of two years, she had only known the streets and her wits had kept her safe, so it wasn't long before she found a cool place underneath a parked car. For a while, she slept and her puppies slept with her.

This dog had not evaded capture all this time for nothing. It was now too hot and too dangerous to be hanging around the bins. She needed to find somewhere cooler and she thought she knew where. Lake Dâmbovița was near the centre of Bucharest and had the advantage of woodland close to the water's edge. In these warm conditions, she would need to keep the pups fed and hydrated. All she had to do was get them across town and to the woods. It was not easy. Taking her time and with the puppies complaining most of the way, they finally reached the woods just before the sun set.

Having checked that the lakeside was not busy she took her pups to the lake where they lapped thirstily. She was so tired by now; she found some dense bushes and got everyone settled and hidden. She had managed to find some fast-food scraps on the way, so her hunger wasn't too severe. The puppies took their fill of milk before falling into a deep sleep.

Her choice had been inspired. Although the lakeside was busy during the day, early in the morning and just before sunset there were opportunities for the mother to scavenge food and all the dogs drank their fill from the lake.

As the dogs grew, she had to find a couple of places for her family to hide together. One of the dogs, the boy with the widow's peak and white socks became an expert scavenger, despite being so small. He was an affectionate boy with deep brown eyes. He became his mother's favourite and major helper.

All good things come to an end and with the summer turning to autumn, the mother turned her thoughts to more sheltered housing. She knew her puppies would not survive a Romanian winter outside. While Socks, as she had named him, kept an eye on his brothers and sisters, she started looking for somewhere warm to get through the cold months.

On her second day of searching, she headed back to her family, tired and frustrated. She thought this task would have been easier. She hadn't noticed the attention being paid to her by the middle-aged lady who lived across from the park. For some weeks, she had been watching the dogs during the day and how the mother went off on her travels. She had also taken a shine to the little male dog who rounded up his siblings. Even so, she knew the dogs would never survive the cold that would soon arrive.

The next morning, with the sun breaking the horizon, the sleeping family never heard the large white van come to a slow stop a hundred metres from their refuge. Three men dressed in white municipal overalls, with large nets and animal boxes crept towards the sleeping dogs. Mumma Dog heard them first and came out of her sleep in a flash. Socks was still groggy and the rest of the family were too slow. Instinct took over and

Mumma Dog made a bolt for freedom, but the third man caught her with the pole (a noose at the end of a long pole). The rest of the dogs were gathered in nets, transferred to boxes and walked towards the waiting van. The middle-aged lady hoped that she'd done the right thing by contacting the dog shelter but the way the dogs were caught made her question her judgement.

What would happen now? Mumma Dog wanted that answering as well. They were all caught. Was this the end?

The dog warden and his helper scooped all the dogs up and put them in a cage together in the back of a van. Released from the net, Mumma Dog counted her pups and with some relief realised they were all together. It was some comfort, but she knew they were in trouble. There was no escaping this.

Chapter 2
A girl and a dog

Almost 1650 miles away, there was another female in a sorrowful state; trapped in her own way and wondering how she would escape her prison. To an outsider looking in, her life was safe and secure. Her room in her parent's house in a quiet town in Northamptonshire was exactly as she wanted it, with the added advantage of an en-suite bathroom.

That outsider would wonder what on earth the young woman would have to worry about, but a passing glance would have revealed nothing of the woman's story and it was tough to hear.

A flexible cast on her right forearm gave a clue that all was not well as was the strange shape on her chest, near her collar bone. When her hair was pulled up in a ponytail a scar on her neck, by her spine, added to the questions one might ask.

Kirsty Ivins, at the age of 39, lived with her parents after many years of owning a house of her own and having lived a life that had taken in trips across America, spells of living in Puerto Rico and many holidays abroad. Now, her focus was on the four walls of her room, the garden and occasional trips to shops accompanied by her mother.

In her younger years, Kirsty had been the literal life of the party. A trip to Germany, when she was 21, had left an indelible imprint on anyone who met her. She could drink all but Oliver Reed under the table and still wake up the next morning, bright as a button. A passion for martial arts had brought her into my world for fifteen months, but by that summer of 2019 I barely knew her. We had only re-established contact two years before; I hadn't heard a word from her for sixteen years.

As Kirsty lived through her twenties and thirties, she developed a knack for choosing waifs and strays as friends and men who thought her boisterous ways were a threat to their beliefs on how a woman should behave. When verbal confrontation didn't calm those ways, fists would follow. It would be bad if Kirsty chose one man like this, but she found every relationship turned the same way. From 2013 to 2017 she found the worst of them all. And worse than that, she hid it from her family and most of her friends and her confidence ebbed away.

By the time she found the courage to leave, and with the help of the police and a few close friends, she had suffered a chronically broken arm, PTSD and her emotions in tatters. One more short relationship went the same way, before her parents moved her out of her house and into theirs. By then Kirsty's home was broken, the new boyfriend was on the run from the police and Kirsty was a nervous wreck.

One positive remained. Her Staffie, Bailey. He had seen the abuse heaped on her and was there to comfort her and to give her someone/something to talk to. The bond between them was as close as any dog and owner could be. Bailey was a rescue that Kirsty had taken in some eight years before and now the dog was getting old. When they moved in 2017 all they had was each other.

Kirsty never had just one name for any animal she owned, so Bailey was also known as 'Pins'. Why? Who knows? That was Kirsty. She told me that when she first met Bailey, he was a bit wonky and she liked that about him. He seemed to be the right dog for her. Quickly they bonded and as he aged, so that bond became ever stronger.

Occasionally he would try and protect Kirsty from the beatings and get kicked himself. When the dust settled and the apologies and denials came, Bailey and Kirsty comforted each other. In the far safer environment of her parents' house, the healing began, but the road was long and painful.

The broken arm became a longer-term problem. When the boyfriend had broken it, he would squeeze or hit Kirsty, so that it never healed properly. After a time, nerve damage developed into Complex Regional Pain Syndrome. This was serious. A broken arm: painful for a time followed by annoying aches and finally healing. CRPS took pain to a whole new level.

It is known as the 'suicide' disease' because it is so painful that patients either take their own lives or have the offending part amputated. It was explained to me as like having your arm on fire and that pain never ends. Many doctors' appointments and hospital visits ensued until finally Kirsty was referred to the pain specialists at Kettering General Hospital. In turn, she was referred to a specialist in Bristol who diagnosed Kirsty with CRPS. This went along with her PTSD, underactive thyroid and depression.

At a consultation not long after the trip to Bristol, Kirsty was told about a procedure known as neuro-nerve stimulator. This involved slicing open her neck and inserting a paddle (like a plectrum) into the vertebrae of her spine, a wire would then be run under her skin to a battery inserted into her chest which would power the electric current to her spinal cord. This would be controlled by an iPhone loaded with specialist software which would enable the current to run through her spinal column into her right arm and deaden the feelings of pain, similar to a TENS machine, but actually part of your body.

Although it sounded like an episode of the 'Six Million Dollar Man' Kirsty agreed to have it done. If the operation went wrong, she could have been permanently damaged and in even more agony. Fortunately, it went right and all was well for a while, then suddenly after seven weeks, the pain came flooding back. She later learned that the paddle hadn't been fixed properly into her spine and had come loose.

She would need the operation again. Kirsty was crushed.

Back on liquid morphine and morphine tablets to control the pain, she would have good and bad days. At night she was plagued by nightmares of the abuse and would often be found in the garden in the early hours of the morning stoking fires in the barrel her dad had for burning rubbish.

In May 2019, life kicked her again. By now, Bailey her waddling, lovely dog was aging badly and the vet told Kirsty that he would be better off being put to sleep. She had known the day was coming but didn't want to face it. Now there was no choice. Kirsty held her beloved Bailey as the vet administered the injection that took his pain away and left it all in Kirsty's heart.

Nothing could touch that pain, not even the wine and spirits she drank to dull the world. Kirsty retreated deeper inside herself and it was hard to see her coming back.

Chapter 3
Books

When Kirsty began her ill-fated relationship in 2013, I had just turned fifty years old. It was a year when I accepted I was now deep into middle-age and wanted to try new things. I did a tandem parachute jump (I found it mildly interesting and good for a story with friends), I continued teaching martial arts and in November that year wrote my first book. Called *The Magic Number*, it showed how to advance your life ninety days at time. I had tried to write books in the past but could never finish them. This time I did. Written and published in four weeks it was a monumental workload in a brief period of time. A book launch to 500 people (off the back of someone else's event) led to selling most of the first 100 copies. It was time to write another.

'*How to seduce your wife (or anyone else's)*' led to coverage in national newspapers and radio and a fantastic book launch and jazz party with a Masque theme. It also led to a business partnership with Caroline Snelling. The company we formed was called 3P Publishing and developed into a business that lasted eight years and published 100 books from seventy authors.

I ran this alongside my martial arts business based in Kettering, ten miles away from 3P's office. The fortunes of this business ebbed and flowed but always remained my passion. Martial arts defined me.

In 2015, I lost my teacher and mentor, Grandmaster Cacoy Canete who lived to the grand age of 96. This was upsetting, but not a major surprise. 96 years is a hell of a life.

The following year in November, I launched my third book '*Punching Above My Height*' (a book about martial arts) with the chief guest being my friend and teacher, Richard Bustillo (a former student of legendary martial artist and movie star, Bruce Lee). I had been learning from Richard since 1990 and he was a major influence on my life. The book launch and seminar he taught were significant successes and when I saw him in the early morning of 14th November 2016, I had no idea this was the last time.

On 30th March 2017, he passed away with liver cancer. Until six days before, no one knew he was ill. He had kept it hidden from his family, even his wife. I was caught off guard and taken by surprise. When I heard the news that he had died I cried my heart out. I did manage to get to his memorial event in Los Angeles; his funeral had happened privately, but the memorial drew a thousand people.

I came back to England determined not to let his legacy die and to promote his teachings for ever more. In the fifteen months that Kirsty trained with me, she attended Richard's 2001 seminar only two weeks after 9/11. She also met Cacoy during his last UK seminar in 2002. The links we had were criss-crossed throughout my life.

Later during 2017, Kirsty first contacted me through Facebook and by then she was going under the pseudonym of Krystal Clear and at first, I ignored her request. I thought it was one of those Russian bride scams. It took her three messages before I was convinced it was Kirsty. For the next year or so we would exchange Facebook messages, but I was in a relationship and I thought her far too young for me as well. There were eighteen years between us.

In January 2019, I taught a women's self defence course and Kirsty had said she would attend, but couldn't physically take part because she was injured. I was intrigued but thought very little of it. Come the day of the course when I was booking everyone in, a rather frail lady entered the martial arts centre and said 'Hello, I'm Kirsty.'

The difference between the young, athletic woman I'd taught and this shaky, nervous person now standing in front of me couldn't have been more different. I didn't recognise her, then I looked directly into her eyes and there it was. Kirsty's face peered out, a hint of a smile breaking through.

'Of course you are,' I said and led her to one of the chairs by the mats. Kirsty explained that she would be making notes throughout and could I not include her in any photos taken. I agreed and I started the course. It ran for three hours and occasionally I would check on her or she would ask me questions. The energy of the group was good and time passed quickly. It was a couple of years later that I learned that Kirsty's mum, Ellen, sat outside waiting to take Kirsty home if at any point she felt overwhelmed. She did fine though and made it to the end. As she left, we said that we would stay in touch more often and we pretty much did. It would be eighteen months before I saw her again and by then her world had changed, so had mine and critically so had the entire world.

Chapter 4
Triangle complete

Mumma Dog, Socks and the other puppies were in a cage all together and that was about as good as it could be. She was philosophical though. They had shelter, water and they were fed twice a day, but she kept an eye on all that was going on. It seemed to her that dogs came and went all the time. None seemed to be there very long and that was what worried her. How long before they were moved on as well? And where did the dogs go?

What she had no clue about was that her little family were now in one of Romania's kill shelters. The longest time that any dog had there was a month. Most only got two weeks. There were two ways out of the shelter. Either they were rehomed with one of the rescue charities or they were euthanised. You walked or you died. That was it.

Obviously Mumma Dog had no way of knowing that, but she also didn't know that her family were one of the lucky ones.

Many Romanians have a callous attitude to dogs and to street dogs especially. With over 60,000 dogs roaming the country I suppose that it is logical that not everyone loves the dogs the way most of the readers of this book will. Fortunately, there are other Romanians who are passionate about saving as many dogs as possible. One of these is Laura Calugaru. She runs a shelter outside the centre of Bucharest and she is the unsung hero of this tale, for she is the person who took in the family. All of them went with her to her shelter. There they were wormed, defleaed and inoculated. Their pictures were taken and the dogs were all put up for adoption.

One of their adoption partners is the charity A Promise to Felix and this is where Kirsty and Sabat's journey together began.

When Bailey died in May, Kirsty spent a miserable summer without a dog. Her next door neighbour had a huge black German Shepherd and she poured her affections onto him, but it was never the same as having your own animal. As summer turned to autumn, fate stepped in and dealt Kirsty some decent cards for a change and wheels began turning that would see Mumma Dog and her pups saved from the worst way out of the shelter.

One day Kirsty was walking through town when she saw a lady with a gorgeous tan coloured dog. They had seen each other previously, but Kirsty hadn't met her dog before. When she learned that his name was also Bailey, the conversation progressed. Bailey was a rescue from Romania and she had got him through a charity called 'A Promise To Felix', based in Northamptonshire. The lady was called Carly and she gave Kirsty the charity's contact details. Kirsty was on their website as soon as she got home. When she had got up that day there was no intention of getting another dog, but this was the day that things kicked into gear.

The site had about twenty dogs at the time, but none grabbed her attention immediately. It would be a couple of weeks before the 'one' appeared. Big eyes, a widow's peak, tiny and extremely cute. A red lead was trailing from a collar around his neck and the little dog was looking up. In another photo he was looking at the photographer, big brown eyes drawing you in with a hypnotic stare. Everything about him said 'save me'. In that moment, Kirsty knew he was going to be her next dog.

That dog, of course, was Socks, not that Kirsty knew that was his family name.

Kirsty was an animal person. When she was younger, her parents had lived outside the town and all manner of animals became pets. Sheep (that she would let in the house), cats, chickens, dogs and there was a small horse as well that once surprised Ellen when she looked up and found that Kirsty had brought it into the kitchen. She could catch birds out of the sky and when she later suffered from nervous shakes, her hands would be rock steady when handling an injured bird. Animals understood Kirsty and the feeling was reciprocated.

Once she had made her decision, things moved fast. Michele from A Promise To Felix made an appointment to visit Kirsty at home, but by then arrangements had already been made to bring the dog to England. Fees were paid and a name chosen for the little brown-eyed dog. He would need this for his pet passport. Kirsty called him 'Sabat'. There are lots of Baileys, Poppys, Daves and an occasional Keith, but to my knowledge there is only one Sabat. The Romanian pup had no idea he was to leave his homeland.

He arrived around 5am on Tuesday 19th November 2019. He was dopey (they drug the dogs to help them deal with the long journey), he smelled of chemicals (like walking through a hospital) and he was scared. Kirsty bathed and dried him and fed him a little meat. Water was readily available and his bed was all made. He was overwhelmed with curiosity and set about snuffling through the kitchen and other downstairs rooms. Soon though, both he and Kirsty flagged. It was time for his first sleep in his new home.

Those early days were difficult. Poor Sabat had only known the streets and the holding cages. When he needed the toilet, he went wherever was available. Learning that the living room and the kitchen were not suitable places took some time. He was a smart puppy though and within two weeks he was fully house-trained. He's a funny dog now as well. If he can find a place to hide to go to the toilet, he will. Which can be challenging trying to pick up sometimes as he has a fascination with defecating on sticks and stinging nettles.

It's fair to say that he loved the garden that came with his new home. He sniffed every blade of grass, every flower and every rock. He would have zoomies dashing around the place like a banshee. He had so much energy and never seemed to get tired. That suited Kirsty's personality as well. Often the pair of them would be up late into the night, hunting around the garden where Sabat would find frogs, the occasional squirrel and hedgehogs. One night, he got too inquisitive and got his nose spiked by a hedgehog. Forever after, Kirsty called them 'Ouch Mouse'. The frogs didn't fare too well, as Sabat was a clumsy playmate and didn't understand that if you threw a frog into the air, they didn't respond well to hitting the ground. The poor dead frog would then have an enquiring paw placed upon its head as Sabat tried to get it to play again.

As Sabat grew larger and stronger Kirsty took him further afield. To be precise, exactly in the fields. Here he could roam off lead and sniff and snuffle around the hedgerows and ruts of the farmland. Often the pair of them would be gone for hours at a time; Kirsty chatting away to her new best friend. In turn, Sabat was slowly learning English and would respond to commands. It took a while though. Alas, Kirsty didn't speak Romanian. At least by the time he became my responsibility I didn't have to teach him the language, but it would be a long time before he responded to me as he did Kirsty.

In January, Sabat was popped off to the vets to ensure there would be no more baby Sabats. Kirsty was told to keep an eye on him for the rest of the day as the sedative was quite powerful. No one told Sabat though and as soon as he got home, he continued to be a hooligan.

Four months after his arrival, Sabat was living his best life. Breakfast and dinner, his own bed, toys, treats, two walks a day and a big garden to explore. Kirsty's dad kept asking why the dog was getting so big. 'I've no idea,' Kirsty would say, but at the same time, hoped he would stop growing soon. She had been told that he'd only grow to the 'size of a small dog, like a Spaniel.' Sabat just kept growing. He's not a big dog, about the size of a Collie, but definitely bigger than promised.

He became close friends with Jack, the huge Alsatian next door although Sabat would occasionally get pinned down with a giant black paw. It was through this type of play and being in the cages in Romania, that Sabat developed his social skills interaction with dogs. He does have a fault though. He thinks that every other dog wants to play as well. That's often not the case, which has caused 'handbags at dawn' situations.

In March 2020, the first Covid lockdown was announced. There were many restrictions, but they barely seemed to bother Kirsty and Sabat. They were in their 'bubble' and Kirsty met hardly anyone anyway. The long walks continued as did the late night bonfires and the searching for 'Ouch Mice'. Sabat had learned not to get too close. It was around this time that Kirsty and I began to communicate more often.

Throughout April and May people began to get used to the restrictions. I have to confess that I enjoyed the supermarket limits. Space at the checkouts was great. No one trying to pressure you into trying to pack faster and people being civilised to each other. At least that's the way it was in Tesco. In Asda, the Walmart folk were out in force. Nothing goes together quite as well as Crocs and too tight shorts and a posterior not designed for them. I was reminded of one of my favourite jokes. 'Sainsburys really is the best supermarket. Do you know why?' Often followed by blank looks. 'Because they keep the riffraff out of Waitrose.'

I began to post daily videos. I think my craving for personal validation was kicking in. I'd talk about good manners in the supermarket. How quiet the roads were. The challenge of running a business from a spare bedroom, when you've been used to daily interaction and an office to go to. Those sorts of things. For some reason, my ramblings started to draw a favourable response. People would message me on Facebook or send me emails saying that they looked forward to my daily video. I was somewhat surprised. However, it also led to an upturn in the messages I was receiving from Kirsty, which was a very good thing.

With so much gloom around at this time, and for a while, genuine fear (no one understood Covid back then), the weather did play ball with April and May being mostly warm and sunny. It was only in June and with the easing of restrictions that the weather turned more showery.

For Kirsty, there was her 40th birthday to celebrate. Life begins and all that. She spent the summer solstice with the sister, Lisa and friends, doing mostly pagan things, dancing under the moon and generally having a good time. By now, Kirsty and I were making plans to meet and it took me a while to realise that Kirsty couldn't drive. Prior to her broken arm and later symptoms of CRPS, she had her own car, but the weakness in her arm meant that driving was no longer an option. That loss of freedom played heavily on her. For me that was no problem. I told her that I'd go and collect her and take her back. She only lived twenty-five minutes away.

Which brought us to Saturday 4th July. We had arranged that I would collect her at 1pm, but I was fifteen minutes late. I found the address, parked on the drive and walked up to the house. There was a covered entrance before the front door with boots, shoes and a bookcase. I rang the bell. I waited a moment and there was Kirsty. Looking so much better than when I had seen her at the self defence seminar in January 2019, although she was nervous and her right hand trembled slightly. There was a brief introduction to Ellen and Sabat appeared, all bouncy and welcoming, but before I had a chance to be properly introduced to him a French bulldog and a Staffie appeared from nowhere, like extras from 'Lady and the Tramp'. They had escaped from a neighbour's house. Kirsty knew the dogs, so we escorted them back to whence they came. From the off, dogs were to be part of our life.

The drive back to my house was easy as we chatted about everything and nothing. It was only when we reached home, that we realised that we had never been alone together. This we found unusual and it was as if we needed permission to be alone, but from who we didn't know. Two middle-aged adults acting like teenagers. I made her a drink and showed her around, lingering in the library I had back then and which we had discussed so many times. She searched through the shelves occasionally picking out a book and delving into its pages. We talked and talked, especially about the martial arts days and discovered that we were mutually attracted all those years before. In 2001, Kirsty was engaged to an American serviceman and I in a long-term relationship. Besides which, surely there were too many years between us. And then, with no one to say otherwise, our relationship began.

A few hours later I was dropping her back at her home. The nervous girl I had met some hours before had been replaced by someone calmer and more in control. As she got out of the car, she put her head back in and said, ‘Will I see you again?’

‘Obviously’, I replied. ‘Am I not too old for you?’

She cackled, as she was wont to do. ‘No,’ she said definitely. ‘I’ll send you a song.’ Which she did and that was the first Garth Brooks song I ever heard. We arranged to meet again the following week.

Chapter 5
Garth and the gang

Until I began seeing Kirsty, my interest in country music was limited. Glen Campbell, Dolly Parton, the country music as sung by Elvis, Johnny Cash; that was about it. I didn't know about modern country. Kirsty opened it all up to me. Luke Combs, Chris Stapleton, the Zac Brown Band and Joe Nichols and many more were all introduced. I liked the country rock sound, even if many of the guys sounded very similar to my ears. But the world that Kirsty truly opened was to Garth Brooks. I had heard of him, but until that first song, I'd never heard any of his music. I was sold from the start.

Kirsty had everything. CD's, DVD's, books and documentaries on her iPad. That girl understood obsession, so when it was time to be Brooks-educated, I had the perfect teacher. The thing that amazed me was that with all his success you couldn't buy his music in a high street music shop. It either had to be Amazon or direct from his website. Also, he'd only ever toured England once, in 1993. Nevertheless, I had all the access to Garth Brooks I could ever want and Kirsty was happy to share. Bizarrely, the day I wrote this Garth announced that he would be playing Hyde Park, London in the summer of 2026. As I've said before, plenty of strange things happen around Kirsty.

Kirsty had been under the NHS Healthcare team for a while and had a designated occupational therapist who she got on well with, but when I asked Kirsty if she'd like to go out on day trips the therapist was anxious that Kirsty wouldn't be triggered. Loud bangs, multiple simultaneous noises and suchlike could set off her PTSD. However, I assured her that we'd be fine, she could leave at any point anywhere we went and I'd be there to reassure her.

So where did we go first? The West Stow Anglo-Saxon village. This is a recreation of a village that stood on that spot for 230 years between 420 AD and 650 AD. We loved it. It was fairly quiet and easy to walk around. We spent a couple of hours there then decided to go to Mountfichet, near Stansted Airport. This was the next phase in UK history with a Norman Castle and village. It was busier here, but apart from a couple of screaming kids in the restaurant, Kirsty coped fine. It seemed that one of the ways to overcome fears was by dealing with them. Her curiosity also played a big part and she felt safe with me.

This first trip had been so successful that I had a more ambitious plan. I asked her if she'd like to see the real Pooh Bridge, near Hartfield in East Sussex. At the time, I had no idea that Kirsty had been a massive Winnie the Pooh fan since she had been a little girl. If there was anything I could have offered her (Garth Brooks concert tickets, a pot of gold, a new arm), I'm not sure anything would have excited her as much as going to see the home of Winnie the Pooh. Cotchford Farm, where the stories were written and where the author, A A Milne, his wife and their son, Christopher Robin, lived, was a mile up the hill from Pooh Bridge. These days the bridge is managed by East Sussex Council and it is a very popular tourist spot. With such an enthusiastic reaction I made plans. I booked an Airbnb in Plumpton Green where we would stay for a couple of nights and visit Lewes, Brighton and Horsham while we searched for my ancient family ancestors and meet Pooh, Eyeore, Piglet and the rest of the gang.

In the early days of a relationship I have found this is a great way to know if you'll have a future. Go away together. Discover if the person you are planning a life with is a slob, leaves skidmarks in the toilet, doesn't wash up or farts through the night. I'm happy to say that Kirsty passed with flying colours in not doing any of these things. The more time we spent together, the more I found myself falling for this unusual, quirky woman. And she went mad for all the Winnie the Pooh stuff. We also visited Pooh Corner; my favourite tea shop in the world. An amazing tearoom complete with the world's only Poohseum – an area completely dedicated to Winnie the Pooh, in all his guises. Kirsty was one happy camper as we travelled from Pooh Corner to Pooh Bridge and then to the Enchanted Place. She stood looking out over the valley in her red Hell Bunny dress, Pooh bear by her side. I took a photo from behind her as she contrasted against the greens and the blues. Sometimes you just know when you get it right. That day I got it right.

Those few days away convinced me of something else. This wasn't a passing phase. I had fallen in love with this woman and wanted to share my future with her. Even after only a few months I was starting to wonder, what else could there be for us?

Ten days after we got back Kirsty was back in hospital for the second operation to fix the paddle into her spine. If this was done correctly this time, it would change her life (as it was supposed to the first time). She would be largely pain-free from the CRPS and it would be manageable. No more morphine, in either liquid or tablet form.

As before, the operation was performed at the John Radcliffe hospital, this time under the top surgeon. She was only in for a day or so, before her parents took her back to their house. There was no denying that Kirsty was in pain, but she was a tough cookie and bore it well. Days passed and she was recovering well. I visited her and checked on her progress, but after three weeks something went wrong.

Kirsty was feeling groggy and ill. Within a day she was on the way back to the John Radcliffe. The battery compartment in her chest had become infected. Antibiotics were prescribed, but at first they didn't help. It seemed that the wound was becoming increasingly serious. After being in hospital for two days, one of the junior surgeons was trying to persuade Kirsty to have a third operation to clean out the wound and set the paddle again. It was like he thought Kirsty was made of zips and not flesh and blood. She argued vigorously and wouldn't allow the operation to be done until the senior consultant had seen her. The next morning, he came round, examined her and said that the antibiotics were now making a difference. Kirsty had won the battle and would not be operated on again.

By the end of October, she was back on her feet and her fitness was improving. Sabat was getting his walks across the fields and I was getting ideas. The bond was getting closer, like two Maltesers on a summer's day, and Kirsty was spending increasing amounts of time at my house. Sabat was coming on every trip as well. The pup and I were becoming friends. I loved having him around, even though he was clearly Kirsty's dog. He absolutely adored her.

When he first stayed at my house, we brought his bed over and put it in the kitchen. He was having none of it. He wanted the sofa. At first, we told him 'no', but I quickly gave in. If he wanted to sleep on the sofa, I didn't mind. Kirsty bought a dog comb, so we could get his fur off the sofa every day and three increasingly became one.

We had talked a lot about a programme called 'Vikings.' Kirsty was fascinated with Ragnar Lothbrock and his wife, Lagatha. It occurred to me to buy her a friendship ring and as these things sometimes happen, I kept seeing an online company, based in Norway, that were selling Viking rings. I ordered one. Trying to get her size right was hard work but I managed it and the ring was ordered. It took a couple of weeks to arrive. From China. Sneaky buggers had set up a company in Norway, but all the goods came from China. But it had arrived and I was happy.

Chapter 6
Are you joking?

Then another idea started to form. Was Kirsty actually the 'one'? I had lived with Anne-Marie for eleven years and was in a relationship with her for a total of thirteen years. I had lived with others who were lovely, but was now the time to get married? After all, I was now 57 years old; at some point I might need a carer!

The proposal did not go exactly as planned. Kirsty had gone to the top floor at home while I loitered in the library on the middle floor of the three-storey house. I could hear her moving about and I kept wondering, is this the right thing to do? Is it too soon? Do I know enough about this woman? Would she say 'yes'? I heard her coming down the stairs. I was about to find out.

'Kirsty. Come in here, please.'

She entered the library and looked right at me.

'Sit down, please.'

For a moment concern crossed her face.

'I've been thinking about this for a while ...'

Her mouth opened as if to say something, but I reached into my pocket for the ring box I had bought for the occasion. China didn't provide them.

'I know we haven't been seeing each other for that long, but I've thought, I'm getting too old to keep searching. I believe that we have connected so well, especially after the Sussex trip, that I'd like to make this permanent. If you'll have me.

Will you marry me?'

Her eyes bulged in disbelief.

'What?' she said.

'I said, will you marry me, please?'

'Are you joking?' She stayed seated in the black reading chair.

'No. Why would you think that?'

'I don't believe you. Get down on one knee.'

'Piss off,' I said laughing. 'Will you marry me?'

'You being serious? This isn't a joke? Are there any hidden cameras?'

'No,' I said gently.

For a moment, she paused, then she leapt up, flung her arms around my neck and said, 'Yes, yes, yes, yes, yes.'

'Ah good,' I replied. 'We'd best do some planning.'

With that, I slipped the little Norwegian ring on her finger. The friendship ring was now a lot more significant. And I, obviously, hadn't done enough planning.

'I was so worried,' Kirsty said. 'I thought you were going to break up with me. Talk about getting a feeling wrong.'

That weekend was one of pure joy. We were both excited at the prospect, although we had no idea how many people we'd be inviting, where we would be having the ceremony or how much it would all cost. I trusted that the money would be found.

We decided to keep it ourselves at first, so we could tell Kirsty's parents the next day, when I took her home.

We got to Kirsty's parents' house about 4.30pm the next day. They were going about their normal business, but Kirsty asked them if we could go into the living room as we had something to tell them.

Before we reached the house, Kirsty had said to me in the car, 'My dad will say one of two things. The first thing he'll say, "But she's a bloody hooligan." And the second he'll ask if I'm pregnant. Just watch.'

Ellen took one chair and her dad (Christian) took the other. Kirsty and I sat on a small stool about four inches off the carpet, looking up at them, like two six-year-olds. We must have looked bizarre.

I spoke and told them that I had asked Kirsty to marry me and she had said 'yes'. We hadn't yet decided on a venue or a date, but we'd sort that out very soon.

'But she's a bloody hooligan,' Christian blurted out.

'Well, she's my hooligan now,' I smiled.

'Is she pregnant?' Christian asked.

Kirsty looked at me and laughed. 'See, I told you so.'

Once they got used to the idea, they were fully behind it.

But what are the logistics of a wedding? I've never planned one before, but it all came together quickly. First the date. Friday 23rd April – as an author and publisher, what could be better than Shakespeare's birthday? As it turned out, something else. Because of Covid restrictions we would have to put the date back a week, to Friday 30th April. Not quite so romantic as the most significant historical event on this day was the death of Adolf Hitler. Still, every cloud and all that.

To double the irony, had we got married in England, we could have kept our original date. It all worked out though and the venue we chose was perfect. Gretna Green, one mile inside Scotland. The home of weddings since 1754. We chose it because we didn't want a church wedding, nor a registrar office. Neither us wanted a hotel wedding either, no matter how nice it was. We could have got married in the county, but nothing took our fancy, until I looked into Gretna Green. I found a website for the Famous Old Blacksmith's Shop and was sold immediately. Kirsty was also in favour. I sent for a brochure which arrived a few days later and then we paid the deposit and booked our place.

We decided on a small guest list too. Only four from my side and five from Kirsty's, plus us. Eleven in total. I spoke to my parents and as they were elderly, I didn't want them making the long drive. One sister doesn't drive which left only one other. We decided as a group that instead of coming to the wedding, I would bring Kirsty to them once we were married, which is what we did. Five months to plan everything seemed perfect. Just Kirsty's dress, my suit, the best man, the maid of honour and the hotel to stay in then. It would all be fine ...

Christmas came and went along with my 58th birthday. Both were joyfully celebrated. It was lovely to be sharing life with someone I cared about. The only blot on the landscape were the second and third lockdowns as Covid wouldn't give in. This meant that my business was operating online only. That caused issues with the book publishing and the martial arts, but we found a way.

I set up a timeline, counting down different things we were going to do until the final lockdown was over. The first of these was the 4 x 4 x 48. This was a David Goggins challenge (Goggins is an ex-Navy SEAL with a reputation for endurance events) that consisted of running 4 miles every 4 hours for 48 hours to complete 48 miles over the weekend. Kirsty and Sabat would be helping me with this. Sabat ended up running three of the legs with me to complete twelve miles over the weekend. Kirsty helped me with the logistics: food, sleep, clean clothes and support. I slept a total of three hours all weekend and Kirsty slept less. All sleep was grabbed in thirty-minute naps. By the end of it we were euphoric and exhausted and we'd raised money and awareness for CRPS.

Next, British Summer Time began, followed by Easter. Every few weeks there was something new to look forward to. Then the gyms opened and I could get back to weight-training again.

There was the announcement that Scotland would open up the week after England. I think this was Nicola Sturgeon just trying to wind up the UK government and in turn, wound me up as well. I was worried that guests wouldn't be able to change their plans, but no one dropped out.

We had one more issue. My old Toyota Yaris was on its last legs and we needed a new car. I bought one on the Tuesday and it was delivered Thursday morning, the day we were heading to Scotland. This was sight unseen, but luckily it has turned out to be a gem. Another Toyota masterpiece. Makers of the most reliable cars in the world! At 10.30am, we set off for Scotland, but first we had to drop off the pup. He was staying with Carly and Bailey, Kirsty's friend and her dog that had led to Sabat being part of our lives in the first place. For him, the second part of our honeymoon would be spent in Sabat's second home, Ellen and Christian's.

The journey north was blissfully uneventful as I started to remember how to drive. I think my longest journey for about a year had been twenty miles, now it was 235 miles, via the A1. The new car handled well and we arrived at the Gretna Hall Hotel about 4.30pm. It was pristine, it was white and it was perfect. Our room looked out over the gardens. Kirsty's family were in the restaurant when we met them; my guests were in Airbnbs in Cumbria. Supporting me were Noah and his partner, Akeem, while Caroline was attending with her daughter, Gabbie. In the evening, I went for a stroll up to the Famous Old Blacksmith's Shop and wandered around the now closed venue. Friday would dawn soon enough.

You never know when the best day of your life will be, but I was hoping that 30th April 2021 would at least rate highly by the time I went to bed that night. It went well.

Chapter 7
The anvil

I was awake early and determined to fit a run in after driving most of the previous day. I set off out of the hotel, up to the Famous Old Blacksmith's Shop, around the complex and into the streets of Gretna Green. It's a very small place so I circled back round and down the hill into Gretna. My curiosity took me into a discount shopping complex. As it was so early there was hardly anyone around, so I ran looking into shop windows. I was on my way back out of the complex when I was challenged by two security guards.

'Can you tell me why you're in here, please?' the female guard asked.

'Yes, I'm getting married today. I came for a run, the gate was open, so I thought I'd take a look around,' I said. Their defensive stance relaxed. It seemed I wasn't a random maniacal shoplifter after all. They were fine, but still escorted me off the premises. At least I didn't get arrested on my wedding day. When I told Kirsty what had happened, she cackled like a hen.

The morning was all relaxed, but by midday it was time for me to go and Kirsty to get ready. Make up by Lisa, hair as well. Younger sister sorting older sister. Who knew what was going to happen?

I drove off to see Noah at his Airbnb, fifteen minutes away. Which was when I realised that I'd left my razor at the hotel. Bugger. This was resolved by Noah going off to the local supermarket, while I took his dog, Poppy, for a walk. Even though Sabat was miles away, I was still walking a dog.

Poppy is a gorgeous black Labrador, two years older than Sabat and was partly responsible for me wanting a dog. She was so loving and a happy dog, that it began my interest in getting one myself. That and sitting in the publishing offices, watching the dogs go by. I decided I quite liked West Highland Terriers back then. Those are the little white dogs that advertise whiskey. Until I mentioned this to Caroline one day who scoffed at my ambition and said, 'You daft sod; you'll look like you're in The Communards!' The idea was shelved. Nothing happened until Sabat appeared on the scene.

Poppy and I had a stroll, taking in the manure smell as we did so, then went back to the house just as Noah appeared. Once shaved and dressed, we looked the part. A swift drive back up to Gretna Green brought us to the hotel and then to the wedding site. The Famous Old Blacksmith's Shop is a museum as well as a wedding venue, so I had a quick look around, while we waited for the bride, the maid of honour and father of the bride.

The wedding room is plain, simple and perfect. The anvil is atop a plinth, set at waist height. Behind where the bride and groom stand are a series of wooden steps where the guests watch. It is unlike any wedding venue I've ever seen. There was no entrance music, just with a designated signal, Kirsty, Lisa and Christian appeared. In these mad times we were all wearing face masks. It looked like the wedding of the James Gang from the 1880s. At my first sighting of Kirsty, I was stunned. I knew I found her attractive and she was a pretty girl, but that day, she was perfect. I smiled from my heart to my feet and my hair tingled as I looked at her. She released her father's arm and stood next to me. I didn't see anyone else except her and the registrar. We were given permission to remove our masks (only the bride and groom as we were exempt from Covid on our wedding day!) and the ceremony began. We managed to get all the words out, there were a couple of giggles and then the registrar was lifting the hammer and hit the anvil. Clang it went, everyone clapped and cheered and we were now married. We had to sign the register and then we were a legal couple. It felt fantastic.

The guests were ushered outside while the photographer took photos of us in an ante-room where Kirsty held a pretend fountain pen over a pretend register, we clanged another anvil, took lots more photos by a beautiful 18th Century carriage and more photos outside. Confetti was thrown and then it was time to go back to the hotel, but not before Kirsty (now Mrs Gibney) and I were taken on a short, but sweet drive in our wedding car, a white Daimler. It had all gone exactly to plan.

We took more photos in the gardens and by another anvil and then went into the hotel for the reception. There were three other weddings that day, but ours had been the last and we got an annexe room to ourselves. The food was good, the cake cut, speeches given and now it was 9pm. Bedtime for the weary newly-weds. The night was as good as the day and I fell asleep as content as I've ever been.

When you wake up on the first day of any holiday it's a good day, but when you wake up on the first day of your honeymoon, it's bloody marvellous. In the run up to the wedding, Kirsty had not been in the best of health and the effort of the wedding day had made her weary, but she was determined to enjoy herself. Having said our farewells to our families we headed to Birdoswald, a fort on Hadrian's Wall. By now the weather was chilly and dull, but we were on our honeymoon, so any time we told someone we'd just got married, they were so happy for us. I can remember my mum and stepfather the day after their wedding, where people would say 'Hello, Mrs Gibney' to my mum. Kirsty now experienced a similar feeling.

We stayed in two Airbnbs, both nice, but the first one (a 17th Century converted stable building) was incredible. We wished we'd only booked the one place. During the next few days, we visited Carlisle, stone circles, Keswick, Ashness Bridge, Ulverston, Windermere and Wasdale Head. The weather overall was ok, snowcapped mountains in May is unusual but pretty. Beatrix Potter's cottage was cute, despite still being under Covid restrictions.

The journey home was good and being reunited with Sabat was fantastic. He went nuts. Bouncing, chewing our arms and generally telling us off for being gone so long. It was six days. The Gibney family was reunited. It was time to make a life together.

Chapter 8
The adventurers

With Kirsty's arm injury she was, in effect, disabled, although you'd never know it to look at her. That meant she couldn't work: a combination of the CRPS and PTSD. She was under the local NHS mental health care unit, although you'd think she could run a marathon, lift a tree and take down a cow on her own. I would go off to work each day around 7.30am and return about 5pm. Three nights a week I would teach martial arts. Basically, working in two businesses. The publishing company where I shared the workload with Caroline and our employee, Lauren (although she only worked part-time) was one of them and martial arts instruction was the other.

In terms of Sabat, he was really Kirsty's dog and we all got on well. He was quite hilarious, sometimes zooming around the house and the garden. All dog duties fell to Kirsty. She fed him, walked him, cleared up after him and took him to the vets. The one area that was my responsibility was running him. Although, as I was to discover, running with dogs is like being a teenage boy trying to seduce his new girlfriend, except that she has taken you back to grandma's house and every time you try to kiss her (or anything else), grandma pops her head around the door and says, 'Would you like a cup of tea, dear?' 'How is your friend?' or 'Do I know your grandmother?' Anything to stop your amorous advances. Because grandma knows you're a randy toad and her grand-daughter is her pride and joy.

Running with dogs has as many interruptions. Getting into a rhythm? Dog stops for a pee. Got a good speed going? Mad hound stops dead and almost pulls you off your feet. Think he's now got the idea? Trotting along just lovely. Bang. A bush has to be smelled. And peed on. And then he turns around and pees from the other side. Why does he do that? Does he pee vanilla one side and strawberry from the other? I am yet to understand this. And he won't tell me. I would run Sabat three to five times a week and Kirsty would walk him daily, sometimes visiting me and Caroline at the office. Occasionally the three of us would all go out together, but most of the time, Kirsty did the walking and I did the running.

Domestic life settled in something akin to the 1950s. Kirsty did the washing and most of the cleaning and cooking too. She was an excellent cook. All very Truman Show.

We went on adventures as frequently as possible. Isaac Newton's childhood home, Woolsthorpe Manor, was only thirty minutes away. This was where the famous apple tree incident happened. Although the original tree came down in a storm, a sapling, that looked more like an apple tree bush, is in the garden. It was also the first place we sampled the Magnum Billionaire ice cream; it remains a favourite to this day. And that's the nature of marriage. It's the little moments you share. Whether that was being in Newton's bedroom or enjoying an ice cream. That's connection. The shopping trips, sorting dinner or paying the gas bill. That's the drudge. When you love someone, it's the tiny moments that bring you closer together.

In August, we went back to Pooh Bridge and took Sabat this time. The great tree that had stood by the bridge since it was built had fallen in the winter, brought down by a storm, so it all looked a bit different, but it was lovely to go back. In September we booked a holiday near Weymouth, taking in the D-Day museum in Portsmouth as well. Sabat behaved impeccably and had his first experience of the sea. Kirsty kicked off her shoes (she needed no encouragement) and took him into the waves. As long as he was in the shallows, he was fine, but when we took him to Durdle Door where it was choppier, he left Kirsty to it.

We stayed in a shepherd's hut that had a dog bed under the bed we slept in. It also came with a nice bit of land for Sabat to run around in. It was all idyllic. We went to Portland, to meet my great friend, Mo Teague and his wife Jackie, (a woman who makes the most incredible scones) and to the village of Tyneham, abandoned during World War II and the build-up to D-Day. It was like a second honeymoon.

At the end of September, we went to see Genesis in concert in Birmingham. Kirsty had been warned by her therapist not to go, as the noise of the music might trigger her PTSD, but we arrived early and Kirsty grew in confidence as more people arrived. Crowds and bustle made her nervous, but with me she was safe. She loved the concert. So much so, that I booked tickets for Steve Hackett, the old Genesis guitarist, and we saw him in Peterborough doing the prog rock stuff.

We went to the cinema, we had random days out and we took Sabat to as many places as we could. At Christmas, we had the morning to ourselves and went to Ellen and Christian's for dinner. Kirsty dressed in an elf dress and we had our first Christmas together as husband and wife.

The first three months of 2022 were bumper months for the publishing company. At last, we seemed to have cracked getting more customers and January was a record month. After years of struggle, Caroline and I had finally got things in a good place.

For my 58th birthday, Kirsty and I went to London. This was the first time we'd been together and Kirsty's first time to the capital in nearly twenty years. For much of the train journey, she was a very stressed girl. More so than I realised. We visited the Jack the Ripper museum (surprisingly good), then went across to Greenwich. When did it get so expensive to go on the Cutty Sark? We went into the National Maritime Museum and saw Nelson's uniform, complete with offending bullet hole. From there we went up the hill to the Observatory, which was closed. Our final trip of the day was to a Titanic exhibition. I took her photo by the statue of Sir John Betjeman at St Pancras Station and then we were on our way home. For all her fears. Kirsty coped with everything, although the next day she was exhausted.

Just a few days later we went to see Texas at De Montfort Hall in Leicester. Sharleen Spiteri, the lead singer, was on great form and the closing tune was 'Suspicious Minds'; my favourite song. Next it was the second 4 x 4 x 48. This time Sabat did five of the legs with me, racking up twenty miles over the two days. That dog is some athlete. The weather was worse than the year before which made it tougher. I got more sleep than the first time, but Kirsty hardly slept at all. By Sunday evening the challenge was complete and we all felt pretty good.

March continued busy with the publishing company and the martial arts was going well too. We were gearing up for our annual martial arts conference to be held on 1st to 3rd April. Kirsty had been given a new camera by her dad for Christmas and she was looking forward to taking photos and video of the event.

On Wednesday 16th March we went to the John Radcliffe hospital to finally get her neuro-stimulator programmed properly. We went with low expectations. The hospital had been a source of great disappointment for so long, but this time they got it right. The only time I've ever seen Kirsty happier was on our wedding day.

The next day Kirsty was determined to come off the Oromorph and morphine tablets that she'd been surviving on for the past five years. She did so without talking to her doctor and by the weekend she was starting to struggle. This is legal heroin and so the cold turkey approach was affecting her well-being, but she thought this was the best way to do it. It isn't, but I had no idea then.

That Saturday evening, we went to the cinema to see 'Phantom of the Open', a funny tale about the worst golfer to ever compete in the Open Championship. On Sunday, Kirsty did her best to hide her discomfort but did disclose to me that her skin hurt. On Monday, I went off to the office and when I came home for lunch Kirsty was very tired and didn't eat with me. That evening, I took the dog for a run and we settled on the sofa to watch 'Ted Lasso', a show we had found on Apple TV that weekend and binge watched it. We ate choux buns, Sabat intruded and obviously got some, but by 8pm Kirsty was extremely tired. The withdrawal of the morphine was acting on her very negatively.

She took some painkillers and I helped her into bed, before going back to watch TV. I checked on her an hour later and by then she was fast asleep and snoring loudly. This was unusual in that she hardly ever snored at all, but otherwise all was well. I went to bed at 11pm and got into bed. Kirsty was still snoring loudly. So loudly, in fact, that I went to the spare bed on the floor below and went to sleep. I thought I heard her get up and go to the toilet in the night, but perhaps I didn't. When I awoke at 5.30am she was still snoring. I thought this was odd, but thought no more of it.

I went to the gym, had a great workout and was in an excellent mood. After breakfast, I went up to see Kirsty, kissed her on the forehead and left for work. She slept on and still the snoring continued. During the morning, I called Caroline, and we talked about Kirsty's snoring. We both thought it was amusing.

During the day I sent Kirsty three WhatsApp messages, but was only slightly concerned that she hadn't read them by the afternoon. I worked in the office until just past 3.40pm and then set off for home. It took less than ten minutes.

I was home at 3.50pm. When I entered the house, it felt odd. The dog was on the sofa and he was subdued. Not his normal bouncy self. I called Kirsty's name and went upstairs. The house was a three-storey affair with our bedroom on the top floor. Everything was quiet.

As soon as I entered the bedroom, I knew my life had changed forever. Kirsty was on her front, her Winnie the Pooh bear beside her and it was obvious that she had passed away. All day I had been working and my beautiful wife had taken her last breath. She was 41 years old, we had been married less than eleven months and my heart broke there and then.

I remember that day in two ways. Both highly confused and with complete clarity. For a while I kept looking at her. I couldn't take my eyes off her and yet this woman that I'd hugged the night before was now no longer alive. The suddenness and unexpected circumstances threw my entire life into disarray.

There were phone calls to make. To the emergency services, to my closest friends and to my black belts to get my classes covered that night; it was only two hours before I was due to teach. Everyone was perfect and did what was necessary. However, the worst call had to be made too. This was made after the emergency services call and if I hadn't done it quickly, I don't think I would ever had the courage to make it at all.

Phoning Kirsty's mother was the worst phone call I will ever make. What was said, the reaction and what happened next will remain with us. You can perhaps imagine how horrific that moment was.

Within an hour a police officer arrived, then another. Protocols were followed and Kirsty's parents and sister arrived soon after. Within two hours the funeral directors arrived and took Kirsty away. Everyone was shocked. I kept going to the toilet. I couldn't stop peeing, a result of my cortisol filled body. I have never experienced that level of shock before and went into a coma of sorts.

The Ivins family left, Caroline arrived along with her son and his girlfriend and we did some practical things that had to be done. The hours evaporated until it was almost midnight and all that was left was me and Sabat and I was sure that he needed a walk. I put him on his lead and went out into the air. Both our lives had changed forever, although neither of us realised the journey we were about to go on.

Part Two

Broken

Chapter 9
Being claimed

I woke up on Wednesday 23rd March in the single bed in the spare room. On the door there was a name plaque: Kirsty's room. She had nabbed it for herself. It was stacked full of her things. It would be many months before I cleared everything and brought it back to being my house.

Many of my thoughts from this time are mixed and jumbled. I thought I should keep a diary at the time and write things down as they came to me, but I didn't. Instead, you'll get the hindsight view and that's probably enough.

First priority: walk the dog. Even though my mind was a mess I wanted to establish a routine for Sabat. Something to help him make sense of everything, when to me very little made sense.

I found a couple of poo bags and his lead and we wandered down to what I understood was called the 'dog field'. I'd been there with Kirsty a couple of times and had met other dog walkers, but she did most of the talking and I nodded politely. When Sabat and I ran, he was my dog. All the rest of the time, he was hers. The pair of them were inseparable and I kept wondering what was going through his mind. I have since learned that dogs understand death as long as they see it. As long as they understand that the person or animal is no longer alive. They feel sad, but know that death has made its visit. When a person just disappears or abandons them, that's what hurts the dog most. Dogs love their owners unconditionally and when that love is rejected it breaks their hearts. Or that's the way I understand it. Remember, I'm a beginner, not David Attenborough.

The day before I had stuck to my usual routine: awake at 5am, leave Kirsty sleeping, go to the gym, have breakfast, get ready for work and get to the office before 8am. Now it was time for a new routine, but I was just making things up as I went along. How long do I walk Sabat for? What is he used to? Kirsty used to take him at all times of the day. Sometimes for thirty minutes, sometimes for three hours. It all depended on how her CRPS was that day.

I decided that an hour should probably do it. This day I knew was going to be difficult. I had made the hardest phone calls (to Kirsty's parents, to my parents and to Caroline), but there were still so many people to tell. You couldn't just blurt it out on Facebook. Not to the people who knew her.

We walked to the field which was half-a-mile away. Sabat was a sod. He pulled like a Shire horse. All that running I'd been doing with him had given him a barrel chest and strong shoulders. No wonder Kirsty used to say he hurt her arm. There and then I realised one of my first mistakes.

In my mind Kirsty walked Sabat and I ran him. Between us, we had a fit and healthy dog. That was fine for me and Sabat, but Kirsty was suffering and because I was wrapped up in my world, I realised that I'd missed something important. Dog walking is hard work. I also realised that I had missed out on hundreds of conversations. It wasn't that we never walked the dog together. We did, but not that often. After all, I was busy. What a bloody idiot.

This book was going to be called 'Walk The Dog Together' when I first had the idea for it, until I found the title I preferred. However, if you are in a relationship and have a dog, walk the dog together. You will talk about the most random shit. Everything to why is Donald Trump so orange to the origins of the alphabet to how you can make or save money. This happens because you are out of the house. You're walking. You're next to each other. The air is in your lungs, you're away from points of conflict and you are appreciating being with your partner/wife/husband etc. You are enjoying the act of being.

On that first walk I realised so much. Dog walking is the perfect couple activity. Your dog is happy. You're sorting through life and time is fairly meaningless because the time you spend together is priceless. One walk when you can only walk alone taught me this.

As I said earlier, when I turned fifty years old, I decided to do things I'd never done before. One of them was making a parachute jump. I had no problems going up in the small aeroplane with six others strapped to crazy tandem parachutists. There are fewer weirder sensations than sitting between the legs of a man you've never met before as he talks in your ear in an aeroplane you're going to jump out of!

All was well, until the moment we sat in the doorway waiting for the signal to jump. The thumbs up came and we leapt into the empty sky. I was only out of the 'plane for a few seconds when I thought 'I'm not sure I want to do this.' My mind replied, 'Good luck trying to get back in the plane, buddy boy.' We hurtled through the air ...

Walking Sabat that day felt the same. 'I'm not sure I want to walk the dog without Kirsty.' 'Well tough shit on that. She's gone and there is no coming back.' Sabat was now my sole responsibility. For the rest of his days, I was going to have to feed him, walk him, wash him, cuddle him, brush him, love him and take care of his every need. Was I a dog owner or a carer? Is there a difference? There is. As I was to discover, this dog would make me laugh, give me discipline, love me, care for me, challenge me and teach me that there was a lot of life still to look forward to.

This first walk was teaching me so much.

The first lap of the field was pretty uneventful. I let Sabat off the lead, as I had seen Kirsty do, and let Sabat wander around, sniffing everything and peeing on just as much.

At this point I didn't know there were 'on the lead' people and 'off the lead' people. Kirsty was definitely an off the lead person, but Sabat would respond to her, most of the time. So, when she called him, he came back. Not so true for me. I had so much to learn, but I was in a state of almost total ignorance.

Looking back over the years, I wonder if I might have been smarter asking Kirsty's parents if they wanted to take on Sabat instead. However, at the time the thought never crossed my mind and in truth it never became an issue. Chris and Ellen are always happy for Sabat to stay over with them, but his home is with me. He's a lucky pup and seems to feel equally at home in both locations.

As I reached almost a full lap of the field, Sabat spotted another dog and flew towards it. For a moment I was worried, but I felt sure I'd met this dog and its owner before and I was right. The dog was a black Cocker Spaniel and the owner was Lucia Gambosova, a Slovakian national with perfect English, a great sense of humour and an easy-going personality. I was fortunate that she was the first of the dog walking crowd that I met.

The conversation started as so many would over the next couple of weeks. 'I'm sorry to tell you that Kirsty died yesterday. She passed away in her sleep and I'm still in shock.' Those first few days I had to repeat these words so often, as every widow/er must. Unless you've been through it, you will never know how hard it is for the teller of the story not to break down there and then. It's utterly exhausting, but those first few days are the hardest.

One of the toughest was with my neighbour, Emilia. The Madondo family lived almost directly opposite us and Kirsty was great friends with Emilia. The children and Emilia's husband, Solomon, knew Kirsty well too.

After the walk, I went across to their house to break the news. There had been a police car outside my house for a couple of hours the day before and later the undertaker had taken Kirsty away, but I have no idea what vehicle they had.

I knocked and Emilia opened the door. 'Is everything ok?' she asked, suspecting that it wasn't. I repeated the line. 'I'm very sorry to say that Kirsty passed away in her sleep yesterday.'

I got no more out. Emilia threw her arms around me and sobbed large, vocal tears. I just held her. Then she held me and for a while we didn't speak. Eventually we talked for a while then I went back to the house. I had phone calls to make.

Meanwhile, back at the dog walk I had new lessons to learn. On that March 23rd morning I was wearing walking trousers and walking boots, so for a moment I didn't feel the wetness on my leg. While I was talking to Lucia, Sabat had cocked his leg and peed on me. I had been claimed. Lucia pointed that out to me.

A few minutes later Sabat decided it was time for a poo. He went off into the longer grass and I followed him. My first job was to get the poo bags separated as I hadn't done so before I left the house.

Rookie mistake, always open up the poo bags before setting off on a walk. You never knew how windy it will be. On this morning there was a slight breeze, but the green horn dog walker hadn't accounted for that as he stretched his hand out and took hold of the faeces. And stuck his thumb right into the brown, squidgy mess. I'm not sure if Sabat laughed at this point, but he scampered away, satisfied with his morning's work. I wiped my brown thumb in the grass and got the worst of it off and made a mental note to remember to keep my hands away from my face.

While on the subject of dog poo, let's discuss the etiquette. First of all, the assumption is that everyone picks up their own dog's poo. Who wouldn't? I agree, but there are caveats. But first ...

If your dog leaves a pile of steaming poo in a public field, such as the dog walking park or an open park, or on the pavement, outside someone's house, a public trail or anywhere that someone is likely to step in it, pick the damn thing up, bag it and put it in a bin. That's your bin, a poo bin or a public bin. I learned very quickly that there are people who don't do this and there are other people who will pick up the offender's turds. I am one of the latter.

However, if you are in a farmer's field, a wood, a valley or near swampy ground, then what do you do? Some people will say that the rules still apply, but my dog has an incredible ability to hide his turds. He is a chameleon shitter. I have bent down to pick up his handiwork and come up with a pile of leaves, or his favourite trick, puncturing my thumb with a rose thorn. I'm sure he tries to balance a turd on top of a flower stem. In these cases, I have admitted defeat and hoped the insects did their best as quickly as possible.

The other exemption is the runny poo. Dogs do have an ability to coat different substances with brown diarrhoea, as if there is any other colour. But there is. Bright yellow, green, sometimes like a shitty rainbow, but only if you are particularly lucky. In these cases, try and wash the offending putrid mess with a bottle of water or pray for rain. Gentlemen, do not be persuaded to whip out your own water provider and pee it away. A fine and a caution for public indecency isn't worth the disapproving look of other dog walkers. A rain dance at this point, could be appropriate.

The next dilemma was easily solved. What does Sabat eat? Fortunately, there were pre-packaged meals of chicken, beef or lamb, but only enough for about a week. It was at this point that I started to realise the financial implications of an animal. Being Kirsty's dog, she had paid for most of his food and his vet bills. Not that there were many of those. Now everything was down to me.

It was during the next week or so that I was blessed to receive a £100 voucher for Pets At Home by the local dog walkers who knew Kirsty. The news of her passing shocked everyone. I didn't know she was such a part of their community and they hardly knew me at all. Knowing that Sabat's food needs were taken care of for the next three months was a relief and I was overwhelmed by the gesture.

For the next few months this group continued to thrive, but the dog field (as we called it) became an increasing cause of concern. The holes in the fences led to many escapes and close calls on the busy road on the other side of it. There were a couple of nasty arguments between dog owners and then the local valley was reopened after months of it being closed by the builders. With the valley open, I now had somewhere I could walk Sabat every day that was enclosed and safe for him to explore. By the summer, that dog walking group had dissolved. Life, as we know, moves on regardless of whether you are in it or not.

Chapter 10
Sharing the news

I'd been up a few hours already and now it was almost 10am. As stoic as I was trying to be, moments of extreme grief would keep overwhelming me and there were things I had to do and I didn't want to do them including letting a lot of people know the sad news.

This feeling would persist for the next five weeks until Kirsty's funeral. Decisions had to be made and I didn't want to make any of them.

All that time, I wanted to gather up Sabat and drive north as far as I could and find a cottage on the Isle of Skye and stay there until it was safe to show my face again. It took me a long time to work out why I picked Skye, then while writing this book I watched the 1969 film, 'Ring of Bright Water', about an author who lives near Skye with a pet otter. I had seen the film when it came out and clearly it had left an impression on me. I would also discover that the story of Mij the otter was based on real events in the life of author Gavin Maxwell. I felt a kinship with Maxwell and Mij in my life with Sabat. Skye had the level of solitude that I needed. I couldn't face people, I didn't want any questions and I wanted to run away.

It was at this time that I thought of the Queen. The year before, Prince Philip had died and the Queen had to go through the charade of his funeral. This poor woman, who had been married to her husband for 73 years, had to sit on her own because of the mad Covid rules at the time. Her heart must have been broken and she sat in St George's Chapel, Windsor, dressed in black, doing her duty, to her husband and the country.

So, I would deal with my problems in an equally stoic fashion. I'd face whatever was thrown at me. Which is what I did.

First though, how to get through a difficult day?

For many years I have been a member of the business development group, the Entrepreneurs Circle. The summer before Kirsty and I had set up the local group that held monthly meetings. She took care of the admin, took lots of photos and helped me set up the room. I delivered the content and did my best to keep people coming back. As a result, a lot of people knew Kirsty and would need to be told. That wasn't a job I wanted to do, so my first call was to EC HQ and asked if I could speak to the man who ran the business, Nigel Botterill.

I knew that he wouldn't be available in the morning (he never is), but with a faltering voice I asked the person who took the call if he could call me back as a matter of urgency. Within twenty minutes Nigel called. I explained what had happened and I felt the shock in his voice. There wasn't anyone I told at that time that wasn't shocked or devastated. Kirsty had no idea how much of an impact she had on the world.

During the summer of 2021 Kirsty and I had been to the EC HQ to film a video course on how to publish books. The first time we did it, there were problems, so we went back again a week later. Because of this, Kirsty met a good number of the staff and bonded very quickly with the man known as Matt the Butler. His name is Matt and he is the company butler. They do things differently at the EC. I can't remember if she met Nigel though.

What I do know is that Nigel was unbelievably kind to me. He told me that he would call all the people that I knew in the EC, so that I didn't have to make those calls. That took a huge burden off me and brought just a little light into a horrible day.

A few weeks later, when it was Kirsty's funeral (or celebration of life as I called it), Matt the Butler and Jess Hinckesman were there to support me. In short, the entire organisation was wonderful throughout and incredibly supportive.

It was then time for me to let others know. Having acknowledged how tough it would be to call everyone I knew and impart the sad news I decided to film a video and send it out through Facebook Messenger. This had the double benefit of only having to say the words once and be able to get the message across to those who knew Kirsty.

Part of the sorrow of that time was how shocked everyone was. There was no clue that this would happen to her and everyone was floored by it.

The biggest question, of course, is 'what happened?'

Something I never got over was how you could touch someone's arm one day and then suddenly they no longer exist. This must be the same feeling that everyone who goes through a sudden death experience must feel. That could be a cardiac arrest, a stroke, road traffic accident or murder. That person that you love so much is gone and you are left behind wondering what on earth you do now.

That's how quickly your life can change and yet, people sleep walk through the days, tolerating levels of bullshit that no one should put up with. If that resonates with you, please stop and make your life as good as it can be.

As for Kirsty, nothing made sense. One minute she was snoring, the next dead. All I wanted was for someone to explain what had happened. I felt guilty as well. Kirsty had lived with her parents for four years; she lived with me fourteen months and now she was gone. I felt that I'd let down her parents, her sister and her friends. Her nephew was devastated at Kirsty's death.

What could I discover? How could I help?

Her phone was passcode protected and I did try to guess the passcode many times, but kept getting booted out. It would be three months before I finally cracked the code but by then it was only good for a factory reset. It's now my business phone.

Her laptop was easier. She had been using it the day before so it was still in session, but time was of the essence as Google can boot you out of session randomly and you can only get back in with the right password. I gave the laptop to a friend of mine who ethically hacks computers for a living and he found Kirsty's password list. They were all held in the cloud. Something else to consider. They might insist that your data is safe, but data breaches are an everyday occurrence so how safe is it?

Within a few days I could track her emails and I could find where she bought her dog food from, which vet Sabat was with and how up to date he was with his medications. As it turned out, right up to date. There were crazy silly things to discover as well. What dog biscuits did she buy? So, I had to access her Amazon account. It was weird going into things that only Kirsty went into. What were those other biscuits he had and where did she get those from? They are called Mini Markies and they are in Asda and Tesco, but I knew nothing of this world and every day threw up new discoveries.

Even without Kirsty's phone, and I'm glad I never read her text messages or WhatsApp conversations (that seemed right and correct), but I did gain access to her Facebook account and her photos on Google and Amazon Prime and for that I was very grateful. Kirsty was a magpie. She hoarded everything, but it also meant there were multiple copies of everything. I found thousands of photos and hundreds of videos I had never seen. I felt like I was getting to know the private Kirsty. She would take videos of herself singing (she had a delicate and melodic voice), walking the dog, giving safety advice, discussing the area and mooching about the house.

When someone dies, I have realised that the thing I miss the most is the sound of their voice. Kirsty had a lovely speaking voice and like the parachute experience, I couldn't go back. But what I could do is listen to her speak, laugh and sing. For this, I am truly blessed.

Chapter 11
Things you should know

A week after Kirsty's passing, Caroline and I were going to a diner experience in a train carriage near Cambridge. As it got me away from the house we kept the appointment; it was a birthday gift I had bought her.

On the journey over we had plenty of time to talk. Caroline had lost her husband to cancer a couple of years before. It was then that I realised how painful that must have been for her and I was aware of my lack of empathy when it happened. I wasn't unkind, but I didn't understand and now I understood that fact. People generally never talk about death and it remains a taboo subject. That's mad. It's as much a part of life as birth. Both things are certain. To live you have to come out. To die is part of the process. So often people would say, 'I'm sorry, I don't know what to say.' In which case this might be helpful.

Here are a few things you can discuss:

The person who has died. Share your memories or if you never met them, invite the survivor to share their thoughts.

Is today a good day or a bad day? Do they want to talk or not?

Is there anything they need help with? Can you help them?

Things to avoid saying:

'Stay strong.' So many people said this to me and I have no bloody idea what it means. Strong to me is lifting weights. I know what they think they mean, but it is totally unhelpful.

'They are in a better place.' How do you know? Are you clairvoyant? Have you travelled back from beyond the grave? As far as I was concerned the best place was with me and Sabat and now there was a massive Kirsty-sized hole there.

'Everything happens for a reason.' Says fucking who? You think there is a reason that my wife, at the age of 41 died in her sleep? Was it for world peace? To stop the badger cull? To help the financial crisis come to an end? Stop being a twat and reverting to cliches. Learn to speak with empathy and understanding or piss off and leave the grieving to their pain. The actual statement should be 'everything happens because of reasons.' That actually makes sense.

The best thing that anyone said to me during that time was from a very dear friend of mine who asked, 'Are you making any progress?' The truth was that I was. Every day that moved me away from 3.50pm on the 22nd March 2022 eased me away from my deepest pain, although there were still many difficult moments ahead.

As for our drive to Cambridge and the hours we spent together that day Caroline said, 'You never really know someone until they are dead.' That was one of the wisest things I've ever been told.

Caroline also told me about the government scheme that helps financially when someone dies. It's called the Bereavement Support Payment and it is paid to the spouse or civil partner of the deceased person. The eligibility factors are that the deceased has paid National Insurance for at least six months in their working career. The payment is a lump sum of £2500, then £100 a month for eighteen months. I'd never heard of this and applied for it as soon as I got home. When it arrived six weeks later it was a godsend and the hundred pounds a month that followed helped me through the tough times that were to come.

In that first week after she had died, there was so much to do. One of the first things was to freeze Kirsty's bank account. Initially Lloyd's Bank were very helpful. I went into the local branch and told a lady my story. She was empathetic and helpful; the account was frozen and later it would be closed. I was also told they had a bereavement department, but not told where or given a number to call. A few weeks later when I had a temporary death certificate (the final certificate wasn't issued until after the inquest) I went back to the local branch and waited in a short queue to speak to a customer service lady.

'My wife has died. Can I speak to someone in the bereavement department, please?' I asked.

She laughed a little and said, 'They're not here. You have to call a number in Leeds (or wherever it was).'

The bitch actually laughed at me. I was livid. Did she not listen to what I'd said? When you ask for the bereavement department, you're not in the happiest of moods and I may have been naive thinking every branch had people who could help, but laughing? I wanted to punch her right between the eyes. Instead, I remained very English and asked if she had the number. She went off to get it. I've never been back in that branch again.

She wasn't the only one though, as you will see.

Because we don't talk about death, so few people know how to discuss anything around it, so the people you do speak to in positions of authority, on the whole, are insensitive arseholes. The bereaved need all the empathy you can give them. Over time, you learn to live with the pain, and there is humour still in these situations, but people who should know better i.e. those used to dealing with broken people are, in my experience, frequently callous bastards. Which brings me to funeral arrangements and undertakers.

I wasn't the only one suffering at the time. Kirsty's parents and her sister were heartbroken too and dealing with their grief, but we still had one massive job to deal with: Kirsty's funeral.

Chapter 12
Dolly Parton

There were two words I came to detest over the coming weeks: funeral and crematorium. I can't say I like them much these days either. With that in mind, the funeral became known as 'Kirsty's celebration of life.' She was young, beautiful and had been an amazing character, so I wanted to acknowledge that and the Ivins were on board too. In fact, they were astonishing throughout the 'celebration' phase. Ellen and Christian paid for a good proportion of the costs and organised the wake in Wellingborough. I could never have done it without them. Less than eleven months before I'd paid for our wedding. Funds were getting tight.

One of the early decisions we made was that the celebration would be at the Wellingborough Crematorium instead of Kettering. The reason for this was that most of Kirsty's friends and family were closer to Wellingborough, but it turned out to be an inspired choice. It's a reasonably new facility and it is bright with huge windows letting in the light. Kettering, by turn, has always seemed dark to me.

Another early choice was finding a celebrant. I had known Peter Wylie for years and when I messaged him and asked if he'd perform the ceremony he agreed immediately, despite the fact that he'd have to come out of retirement to do so. From start to finish, Peter was brilliant. He met the family with me, gave us great advice and on the day, delivered a wonderful reading and held the whole thing together superbly.

That left choosing the funeral directors. Again, Peter gave us excellent advice on who to choose which is how the Raunds branch of Co-op Funeral Care were placed in charge of Kirsty's final journey. While all these decisions were being made Kirsty was still in the Kettering morgue. With sudden death an autopsy is always performed, but this wasn't Quincy. No theatre production and then the results are given in a few days. Quite the opposite. Kirsty would remain in Kettering for three weeks until she was released into the care of the Co-op, but the full results wouldn't be known until July and the inquest that followed didn't happen until the following April. I was shocked at this. Who knew these things took so long?

In the meantime, Christian, Ellen and I had an appointment at the funeral directors. We had to choose our ceremony. At this point I make my plea to you to plan your funeral now. No one knows when they are going to go, so plan it. If you're with someone, choosing the casket can be hilarious.

'Do you want the one with the pictures from your past on it?' I had no idea you could do this, but you can. It's like a collage on the coffin, like a wrapped flower delivery van.

'How do you fancy a wicker casket?'

'How about a cardboard one?'

And another important consideration. Burial or cremation? It's worth remembering that you usually have to buy your plot first and burials are about £1000 more expensive than cremation.

As I made the drive to Raunds, I was thinking of every excuse possible not to have this meeting, but I owed it to Christian and Ellen and most of all, I owed it to Kirsty. I wanted her to have the best possible send-off and that meant being involved in almost everything.

I was a couple of minutes late and when I arrived, Christian and Ellen were sitting in armchairs facing a lady at a desk. A third chair remained empty. I said my greetings and apologies and sat down.

I'm not going to name anyone, but this was the start of a process that constantly annoyed and upset me. On the celebration of life day, the undertakers were amazing and most of the background staff were too in the interim, but the lady who dealt with us was a nightmare. Except when I visited the Chapel of Rest; then she was brilliant. But we got off on the wrong foot straight away.

She began to explain a standard funeral and the costs were creeping through the thousands of pounds. Something else no one talks about: the cost. I asked the lady if she had a brochure we could look through.

'Didn't you see the email I sent you? The brochure was attached,' she explained.

'In my head I said 'Don't be bloody ridiculous. How am I supposed to see a funeral director's brochure attached to an email when I'm trying to figure out how to keep people training and feeling guilty at leaving all the publishing work to Caroline?' Instead, I asked for a hard copy for me and the Ivins. Two brochures were produced.

The woman started to go through the options. The main one she tried to sell us was the 'standard option'. I asked what they involved. 'Well,' she said, 'There's the two limousines ...'

I stopped her before she went any further. 'The what?' I said.

'The two limousines,' she tried to say, as if this was all completely normal. 'The one that will carry the coffin and the one for yourself and the family.'

I could see Christian getting annoyed as well.

'I don't think so. I got married eleven months ago and we were in a limousine together. I won't be going in a limousine for her funeral.' And that was the end of that.

The meeting continued and Christian and I did most of the talking. Ellen was too upset.

And that's what pissed me off about the whole thing. All of us were devastated and yet here we were having someone trying to upsell us like we were in McDonald's and someone saying, 'Is that a large fries?'

I don't know if this is what the funeral industry is like usually, but we were all unhappy when we left the funeral home. I think the grieving need more respect.

We got it all sorted quite quickly really. Coffin chosen. Peter met us at the Ivins family home and we talked about Kirsty. The sort of person she was and I said I would write up some of the stories for him to use at the service. Then there was the music. Of course, Kirsty had left us nothing in the way of what she would like, so we picked a few songs and came to a final list.

'TNT' by AC/DC.

'Me and Little Andy' by Dolly Parton.

'Young and Beautiful' by Elvis Presley.

'Friends in Low Places' by Garth Brooks.

And in the middle of the ceremony when a montage of Kirsty pictures would be shown, Lisa and the band she was in recorded an original song called 'Song for Krystal'.

What could go wrong? We come back to our friend, the administrator.

When I put in the music choices request, I wrote them out this way:

'Me and Little Andy' from the album 'Here You Come Again' by Dolly Parton and so on.

Fortunately, there was a problem and I had to call the company that deal with audio-visual presentations for funerals up and down the UK. Obitus is their name and the lady I spoke to was super-helpful.

'Shall we go through your music choices?' she asked.

'Great idea,' I replied.

'TNT' by AC/DC. That was interesting. We had to buy that one. No one has ever asked for that before.'

Kirsty would like that, I thought.

The lady continued.

'Here You Come Again' by Dolly Parton ...'

I stopped her dead in her tracks.

'What?' I exclaimed. 'Where did that come from?'

'This is what is on our list, Mr Gibney,' she said.

'I don't think so. 'Here You Come Again,' at a funeral. 'What's next? 'Caspar the Friendly Ghost? Kirsty would have found that hilarious, but we'll stick with 'Me and Little Andy.'

So next, we should have 'Young and Beautiful' by Elvis Presley.'

'No,' she said. 'Jailhouse Rock' by Elvis.'

For a moment all went silent.

'Are you kidding?' I said, voice raising. 'At a funeral? Jailhouse Rock?'

By now I was convinced that Kirsty was involved. She would be finding this absolutely side-splittingly funny. Imagine sitting there and we have 'Here You Come Again' and then while we recovered from that, Elvis floats out of the speakers with one of his most popular rock n roll songs. In my mind, I could hear Kirsty cackling away. 'There you buggers,' she would have said. 'Take that and party.'

We went back through the list again and got it all sorted. Imagine though, celebration of life? It would have descended into farce and I think Kirsty would have enjoyed that.

Before she died, I was a total sceptic. Once you died, that was it. No more. A puff of smoke or worm food; that was your choice and then it was time to get on with life.

That wasn't my experience.

The first thing to deal with was the house. She died in our bedroom on the top floor and for a week I couldn't face sleeping in that room. The mattress, sheets and bed clothes had all been replaced, but to me it was a heavy deal. For almost two years we had slept together each night and awoke to each other's faces. In the grand scheme of things, it wasn't a long time, but it was intense. We lived life. We did things. We laughed a lot together in that room. And it was full of her things. To deal with the loss I was going to have to turn the house back into my home and not our home, but how did I do that and still be faithful to her memory? It was a tricky road to negotiate. The answer was to do it all gradually. Only throw away the obvious things. Anything that might have a connection, store away and review at a later date.

Caroline came to my rescue again. She told me that she had a friend whose husband had passed away and she found it difficult to cope with any memories of him so threw everything out. About a year later, when she felt more at ease she was desperately upset because all the physical reminders of him had gone. I found that incredibly helpful.

As time moved on that's what happened. Keep some things, throw away the things I definitely didn't have a place for or give them to people who could make good use of them.

I'd read about signs that the dead were still around, specifically white feathers and robins. They would turn up regularly and I took notice and said 'hello'. I also spoke to Kirsty as if she was still here. I didn't know if she could hear me, but I reasoned that if she could it was lovely and she would know how missed she was and if she couldn't hear me, so what? I felt better for talking anyway.

Death was changing me.

First time around
September 2001 with Richard Bustillo

The photo that captured Kirsty's heart.
Sabat in Romania

Arrival in England – 19th November 2019

The loonies – March 2022

Wedding day – 30th April 2021

The look of love

'But Dad, that looks good.'

Sabat doing his thing for the Dorset Tourist Board.

Some memories you never forget

With comedian Jimmy Carr – September 2022.

Sabat and mum – March 2022.

Dog Walking for Beginners - 2025

Chapter 13
Kirsty's Korner

Every year I host a martial arts conference where students gather from across the UK and some from Europe as well. This was happening on 1st to 3rd April, only ten days after Kirsty had passed. I dare say that no one would have blamed me if the event had been postponed, but I also thought that Kirsty would want it to go ahead. She had been looking forward to it and was getting all her cameras and memory cards set. I also thought that this would be the perfect opportunity to remember her in an environment that she loved and to people who knew her.

With that in mind, I contacted my usual printer who said they could get a canvas printed if I could get the artwork to them in time. I set about looking for photos and then collated them. The printers made some adjustments and had the canvas ready as promised. Bless them, they wouldn't take any money for it either. A lovely gesture.

The first day of the event was quite a sombre affair, but I tried to set the mood and told everyone that I wanted the weekend to be a tribute to Kirsty and that everyone who knew her should honour her in their own way.

On Saturday 2nd April, I gave a speech and unveiled the canvas. We also retired her sticks which now hang on the wall along with her nunchaku and Kirsty joined Richard Bustillo as a focal part of the martial arts centre and we now had 'Kirsty's Korner'. I really don't remember much about that weekend and delivered most of my material on autopilot and hoped that everyone had a good time.

I was teaching on autopilot a lot during those days and all of it now seems like a fog with certain events standing out like a mountain range above the clouds.

It was around this time that I realised that even in profound sadness, unusual circumstances occur.

I tried to return to work at the publishing company too early and three weeks after Kirsty died, I had a meeting with two authors in regards of a book we were going to publish. This was at The George in Stamford, Lincolnshire. As I came out of the meeting, my phone rang and it was the administrator from the funeral directors.

In my mind, I wanted to see Kirsty again before she departed the Earth forever.

'Mr Gibney?' the lady enquired.

'Yes,' said I.

'It's Co-op Funeral Care, in Raunds,' she said. I thought unnecessarily to be honest. It wasn't like I had a batch of wives that needed their help.

'I'm afraid you won't be able to see Kirsty.'

'Oh, why is that?' I was deeply disappointed.

'Well Mr Gibney, she has come back from the hospital and she's quite dehydrated.'

'I'm not surprised,' I said. 'She's not had a drink for three weeks.'

The line went quiet for a moment. She made another apology and then rang off.

The next day she rang again.

'Mr Gibney?' She sounded more cheerful this time.

'Yes?' I faltered.

'I have good news. You can see Kirsty after all.'

Now I was confused. Had Dr Frankenstein been in and wired her up?

She explained that the embalmer had been in and said that he could help Kirsty look presentable. At this point I was wondering if they'd lost her head.

'I need to speak to him. Can you get him to phone me, please?'

She agreed she would.

Five minutes later my phone rang.

'Hello Mr Gibney,' he said, 'It's Mark the Embalmer.'

'Honestly mate. You need to work on that introduction.'

We chatted for a bit and he explained that he could make Kirsty look well enough that she could be seen. This meant another awkward phone call, the day before after the administrator's call, I had to tell Ellen that we wouldn't be able to see Kirsty and now I had to say that we could. This was better though. As macabre as it might sound myself, Ellen and Christian all wanted to say our final goodbyes.

The date for the celebration of life was set for 26th April 2022 at 2pm. Before then, I went over to the crematorium to look around and was given a tour by a lovely man who ran the place. It all helped me approach the fateful day.

On Wednesday 20th April I made another of those drives that I didn't want to take, this time to see Kirsty in the Chapel of Rest at the Funeral Home. By now my album of choice was Bruce Springsteen's 'Born To Run'. Those eight tracks resonated with me on every journey, but the saxophone solo by Clarence Clemons on 'Jungleland' moved me almost to tears every time I heard it. Bruce helped me through. A year later I would see him at Villa Park in Birmingham and those songs would be sung live. For many reasons 'Born To Run' is a special album and now it means a bit more to one other person in the world. Me.

This time the administrator did her job well and prepared me for how it would be. The room was kept at a low temperature as

Kirsty still had six days before her celebration of life and even though she had been embalmed there would still be some changes over those days. Mark the Embalmer had requested that I provide the clothes for Kirsty, so I chose her red and black dress with cats on it that she wore when we first went to Pooh Bridge and she also wore at Warwick Castle. On her feet she had a pair of red and white Converse. Kirsty loved Converse. I also added one of her Winnie the Pooh bears to keep her company.

I went into the small room and there was Kirsty's coffin on a support called a bier and a chair by the side of it. On a table was a box of tissues ready for the tears that would come. Looking peaceful and asleep was my wife. I had chosen to see her this way, but it was like diving into freezing cold water. For fifteen seconds or so I couldn't breath and as I hyper-ventilated, slowly I calmed down and then I cried. Hard tears that rolled down my face and hurt my throat. To know that this woman had looked devastatingly beautiful almost a year before as we stood by the anvil together in Gretna Green and was now in her final prone position broke my heart all over again.

I stayed in that room for fifteen minutes, talking to Kirsty and telling her my plans for her celebration. I told her how the world was broken that she was no longer with us and how Sabat was coping. When my time was up (I could have stayed longer, but emotionally I couldn't) I left, thanking the administrator and went to see Kirsty's parents.

They had been to see Kirsty earlier in the day, but there wasn't much to say really. What could I say? I was still feeling massive guilt that Kirsty had died on my watch.

Two days later I went to see Kirsty again. This time it was odd. I felt nothing other than peace at being with her. It felt strangely 'normal'. I was supposed to sort some flowers that day with a florist in Raunds, but she had been called away and I had to make another visit the following morning. I felt melancholy when I went over this time and felt even sadder as I walked past the funeral home that was now closed and I couldn't go in, but knew that Kirsty was lying in there.

As I wandered across the road, into the memorial gardens, I met a strange woman who spouted some almost unintelligible gibberish about being a vegetarian but not wanting to kill herself. As bizarre as it was, it broke my mood and deflected my thoughts. Did Kirsty send me a loony to make me feel better? Sceptics will cry coincidence; spirit believers will assure me that she did. I was just grateful for the laugh.

On Monday I saw Kirsty for the very last time. This time I was broken again. These feelings of grief were impossible to control. I often felt like I was one step away from total collapse, but I kept putting one foot in front of the other. Like Robert Falcon Scott, in one of my favourite films, 'Scott of the Antarctic'. One painful step at a time, but I was going to survive.

From January 2022 until August 2023, my life seemed to be full of funerals. Kirsty and I went to the funeral of Richard Swindall, a lovely man I met during the fight to keep Thrapston library open. He was 90 when he passed away. The next funeral we attended together was hers. There was also Jeff Gonsalves in August, Sherrie Cooke in October, plus two authors we'd published who lost their wife and daughter (separately) and my great friend, Lincoln Noel, lost his wife to cancer in January 2023. It seemed to be never ending and finally in August 2023 another friend and student, Kimi Armstrong also passed due to cancer at the age of thirty. Kimi was a friend of Kirsty's and had been a student of mine for more than ten years. It was as if

Mother Nature was telling me I would get used to death soon enough.

One of my favourite tv series is 'Yellowstone'; the modern Western starring Kevin Costner. I bought a magazine dedicated to the show and in there was an interview with one of the main Native American actors, Moses Brings Plenty. He said that in the Lakota Sioux language there is no word for death. Instead, they believe that life passes from the physical stage to the spiritual phase, without pause. I have thought for a long time on this and it appeals to my psychology.

In the Christian belief there is the idea that death is the end of life and then you pass to Heaven, if you have lived a good life. With the Lakota Sioux belief, it helped me to think that Kirsty had passed from one world to another, but was still alive in that way.

If you've never felt that deep sense of loss you perhaps think that I'm a bit doolally and maybe you're right. All you need to know is that thinking this way about Kirsty brought me comfort.

Chapter 14
Winnie the Pooh

I was dreading Tuesday 26th April, but Caroline came up with another gem: 'You'll be fine. On the day, the body reacts to get the job done.' She was right, but there was a price to pay.

When the day arrived, I drove over to Raunds where the funeral procession left from; Kirsty making her final journey from the family home. The lead undertaker approached me on the drive of the Ivins' home and gave me a small brown envelope. Inside were her wedding ring, engagement ring and the friendship ring I'd given her when I asked her to marry me. It also held her necklace. He invited me to see the flowers in the hearse and shortly after, the procession began the eight-mile journey to the crematorium.

Noah and Akeem made the journey with me. No limousine, just the trusty Yaris. When we reached the crematorium, most of the mourners were gathered outside, including my family. My mum and stepdad and my two sisters. I was surprised at how many people were there, well over 100. It was lovely to see my friends and students, but also dog walking friends and members of the Entrepreneurs Circle, including Matt and Jess who worked at the HQ. It brought home to me how supported I was.

We were lucky with the weather and the sun shone through the large window. I had requested that people wear colour instead of the formal black and most people did. One friend of Kirsty's arrived in something resembling a Winnie the Pooh suit. He had also contributed a poem.

On the coffin and by it, the room was with filled with Winnie the Pooh stuffed characters. We had come to celebrate this wonderful woman and over the next forty-five minutes we did. If someone close to you dies, always do your best to attend their funeral and give them a good send off. You might go to more than one of their weddings, but the funeral (or celebration of life) is a one off. It is a unique event, just as being born is. Honour the person. Let others know you cared and most of all, support those closest to the deceased. They feel it.

Peter Wylie was brilliant throughout the ceremony. Lisa, Kirsty's sister, performed a wonderful tribute that started by raising a hip flask to her sister and taking a drink. Friends of Lisa and Kirsty had also been primed. It was a surprise to me, but brilliantly done. It raised the mood immediately.

I spoke my words, carefully chosen and written, a hint of tears and many smiles and the music was perfect. We filed out to Garth Brooks and gathered outside. Everyone was kind and respectful. I know I'm biased, but it was the best final send-off I've ever attended. People spoke to me afterwards and said it felt like a true celebration of life. It had colour and humour, tears, of course, but laughter as well. Kirsty's memory had been well served.

All that remained was the wake that Ellen and Christian had organised and I spent most of that time with my family, but also spoke to others. By 5pm it was time to return home and to Sabat too. He wasn't allowed to attend unfortunately although I'd have loved for him to be there.

The evening has gone from my memory. All my emotions spent.

Part Three

Struggling

Chapter 15
The Enchanted Place

The day after the day.

Funerals are strange things. When you go to someone's funeral you want to pay your respects and learn something about the person. In the summer of 2022, I went to a funeral of someone I didn't know well, but wanted to support a friend who was going. I remember it only because the person we were honouring went to university, went on holiday with his friends most years and propped up a bar in a local pub. That was all we learned about him. It was all done in twenty-five minutes. No one had put any thought into the event and the man's life appeared to be one of quiet desperation. I knew then that we'd performed a great service for Kirsty. She had been honoured and remembered. No one walked away from that event with a feeling of 'so what?'

If you're ever in charge of a funeral for someone, honour them. Make sure they are remembered. Unless they are evil of course, then pour petrol on them. That's one way to make a funeral memorable.

But the day after the day, you don't have anything to focus on after days or weeks of it being the only thing you focused on. Except that wasn't true for me. Four days after Kirsty's celebration of life was our first wedding anniversary. Reading that now reminds me of the utter pathos of the event. The anniversary was on a Saturday, so I requested to collect the ashes on Friday afternoon. I wasn't even sure it was possible, but after the rollercoaster level of service I'd had at the Co-op, they came through and I was able to collect the tubes of ashes.

If you've never collected ashes before, it takes you by surprise. This person you loved, this person who was so real to you just a few weeks before, is now in two containers about twelve inches high and four inches across in a cylindrical tube. It looks like nothing, but then you realise how heavy they are, not like a huge rock, but heavy just the same.

I went to see Ellen and Christian and gave them their half of their daughter. The other half was for me. We'd already discussed what we would do with Kirsty and the first part was to happen on 30th April. Our first wedding anniversary.

For a long time after Kirsty had died, I used to dread Tuesdays. Every week it would roll around and it would get to 3.50pm and my mind would take me back to walking in the bedroom and seeing Kirsty again. Face down, asleep and never waking up. As the weeks rolled past that would slowly fade. Wednesdays weren't a lot better and Wednesday 27th April was the worst.

I don't remember the day at all but as the evening closed in all the emotions of the past five weeks seemed to come together in a shit storm of love, pain, loss, agony, fear and loneliness. I guess I had some sort of panic attack. This wail of despair came up from inside me and the emotional pain became a physical sensation as if my body was being pulled apart by the gravity of it all. I'd never felt anything like it before or since and for a while I was scared. Scared of what my body was going through and my mind as well. How could loss hurt so much? Sabat came to see me, but ran off not knowing what to do. The feeling lasted perhaps fifteen minutes, maybe as long as half an hour. I don't know; but gradually I got my breathing back under control and I sat on the sofa, utterly spent. Exhausted, sad and broken. Sabat returned and sat by me, having no words to say, but only love to give. We went for a walk and not a word was said.

On Friday I collected Kirsty's ashes and the next day headed south to East Sussex and Hartfield. The home of Christopher Robin, A A Milne, the Hundred Acre Wood and Winnie the Pooh. Caroline supported me and helped me through the day. Sabat came along too.

We had some refreshments at Pooh Corner, the best tea shop in the world. I bought some keepsakes to take home with me and we headed to Pooh Bridge. The car park is at the top of a wooded area and you walk down the path on a fairly steep hill. It's all very English, very lovely and on this occasion, very sad. Not at all like the times I'd been before. Then things had been joyous, Kirsty was in her element, finding Owl's house and Piglet's too. All lovingly put together by the council and woodland commission for tourism and joy.

At 4pm on Saturday 30th April 2022, exactly one year on from the moment I stood waiting for my bride in Gretna Green, I stood on Pooh Bridge and thought about that day in Scotland. I was now alone. Whatever happened after this, I would always remember that time, in those places, on that day. An anniversary that would bring me happiness and sadness in equal measure. Caroline stood a few feet away, allowing me to deal with my emotions and preparing to pour Kirsty's ashes into the stream below. Just then a family who had been looking around, in their own time, came within ear shot. Actually, their young son screamed like a banshee. My sadness disappeared in a moment.

'Fuck me,' I thought. 'What am I thinking?'

Of course, Pooh Bridge was a place of pilgrimage for fans of the characters and the books, but not just for adults like us, but for thousands of children. Even when Kirsty and I had visited we had to avoid the little darlings. They were excited. Parents had built the bridge up to be a place of reverence. 'This is where Christopher Robin, his daddy and Winnie the Pooh invented the game of Pooh Sticks. Yes, Mary, it's all real.' Small children would run and scream and shout and make a hell of a noise. In that moment, that five-year-old saved Kirsty from purgatory. She loved Pooh Sticks Bridge when it was quiet and it was only quiet because we visited when there was hardly anyone around. No, she would go elsewhere and I knew exactly the right place for her.

Before we left the vicinity though I did want to leave something of her connected to this place, so I wandered off the path, found a tree and nearby it, buried some Kirsty treasure. A marble, a piece of jewellery and a pebble. It's still there undisturbed and Winnie the Pooh and one of his greatest fans are united in memory, together.

We wandered a little way up the other side of the hill and found Mr Sander's house. (Mr Sanders was another name for Pooh Bear.) I took a small handful of Kirsty's ashes and sprinkled them there, then we headed back up the hill to the car.

We were headed for the Enchanted Place. This is a clearing in the woods that overlooks the valley looking down towards Hartfield and Cotchford Farm where the Milne family lived at the time of the writing of the books. There is a huge stone at the Enchanted Place with a plaque on top of it that tells you that A A Milne and Christopher Robin sat there together. It's your connection to history and it is a beautiful spot. The first time Kirsty and I visited, I got a great photo of her standing looking at the views. This would be the perfect place for her to rest now. I took out her ashes and spread them in the bushes at the top of the hill, just in front of the stone. Looking at her there, nestled in the leaves, was too much for me and I cried for a while. Caroline stood back and looked after Sabat. We waited for a few minutes, just me, Caroline and Sabat then headed back to the car.

Sabat, knowing the perfect way to break any solemn mood, decided this was a good time for a poo. It was at that moment that I realised I didn't have a poo bag. God, I was such an amateur. I did something I never do. I found a large stick, balanced the pile on the end of it and launched Sabat's present into a gorse bush with a shot that Rory McIllroy would have been proud of. Sorry Pooh fans. I'm sure Mother Nature took care of it on this occasion. And I've never forgotten poo bags since.

Sabat came to my rescue again. The perfect reminder that no matter how sad you are, there is always shit to deal with. What a dog.

Chapter 16
Kirsty's surprise

So, that was that, right? Now it was time to pick up the pieces and move on. April had been about organising the celebration of life, the laying of the ashes and finding a new life direction. Is that what happened? Not a bit of it.

There are so many things that people don't talk about with grief and one of them is fatigue. As we go about our daily business, we give out an inordinate amount of energy. We give to our friends, our children, our partners and our family, but that's not all. If someone stops you in the street and asks for directions, that's giving energy. For a start, you're trying to work out if they are going to mug you and when you realise they are actually okay, there's the interaction itself. We give to the friendly shop assistant, to the person serving you coffee, to the driver letting you through. Every day we act as if our energy is limitless and at the end of the day, we are ready for bed.

With grief, that isn't the way it works. At least it wasn't for me. I was exhausted every day. There was only one thing I could do. I could teach martial arts, although even then I know I was an erratic teacher. If anyone wasn't putting in what I thought was enough effort, then I went off at the deep end. I definitely lost a few students then and I wasn't really aware of it happening either. As the year progressed, this became a major problem.

I was struggling to sleep as well. Once I was asleep then I was fine although I wasn't dreaming at all. I have no memories of any dreams for at least six months. It was the getting to sleep that was the real problem.

When Kirsty and I were together we were usually in bed by 10.30pm, asleep within thirty minutes and I was up at 5.30am every morning to go to the gym. After her death, I was finding it hard to sleep before 11.30pm. Sometimes it would be 12.30am or later. I'd still wake at 5.30am but I'd be asleep again before 10am. It was like undiagnosed sleep apnoea. I'd have breakfast, put on the tv and nod off. Combined with the gym and a two mile walk with Sabat and I was gone. You'd think the easiest answer was to go to bed earlier, but my mind wouldn't switch off.

I'd gone back to work at 3P Publishing, but my heart wasn't in it. We still had three or four books still to work on, but I couldn't go back to the office as I had Sabat to look after and I couldn't bear to leave him on his own for eight hours a day, so I was working from home. That meant I'd lost the daily interaction with Caroline and all the routine that entailed. By May, we had decided that it was time for 3P Publishing to close down. I would concentrate on the martial arts and Caroline would find a job, when she was ready.

We did one more book launch on 7th May for Reef Stone (real name Tony). He had been so supportive of me in the previous two months, so I agreed I'd MC the event and Caroline helped him with the sales. It was done at a coffee shop close to where I lived and only lasted a couple of hours. I put on my best false smile, did my performing monkey act and acted as if all was normal. It wasn't. By the time I got home, I was done in. The launch was on a Saturday night and it took me all day to recover to take the classes on Sunday night.

What I could cope with was spending time with close friends. I went on a couple of days out to Stratford-upon-Avon and London and tried to find my place in the world again. Long dog walks with friends helped too, but no matter how hard I tried, I was lost. I had put all my eggs in the proverbial basket with Kirsty and had plans that would make our life wonderful. I felt like we were newlyweds (which we were) and we were learning about each other. I worked too hard, didn't notice when she was stressed and was not the best husband I could be, but I loved her deeply. She made me laugh, she was lovely to look at, Sabat was the glue that cemented us together and we had a future. Now all I had was Sabat and for now, he would have to do.

And while all this was going on, there was still all the 'sadmin' to sort. There is a Government portal that allows you to deregister someone from the official existence they have: driving licence, passport, National Insurance number, bank accounts, blue badge number, all those sorts of things. That made life easier, just the one place. The thought that you were making someone you loved disappear was difficult. For forty-one years, Kirsty had been part of this spinning planet but not anymore. Looking at it logically some years down the road it's all obvious, but when you are fighting their disappearance (I suppose that's the denial stage) it's much harder.

One thing I have kept going is her Facebook page. Her mum and I discussed this and we agreed that we wanted to keep her memory alive, so we haven't put her page into memoriam. Occasionally her sister will post memories as I do too. At first, I used to publish unseen photos of Kirsty but then I'd get messages from some her friends saying I was being disrespectful. I politely explained that I'd discussed it all with Ellen and I would carry on. Never as Kirsty, but on Kirsty's page. And I would ask one question. 'Did I meet you at the funeral?' I asked that of every person who messaged me who said they were a friend of Kirsty's, so I thought 'Well, surely they would have been paying their respects.' None of them replied and none of them ever messaged again. Over time, Kirsty's friend count has decreased, but there are still the hard core respecting her memory and making the occasional comment. I do understand as well. I have removed myself from some friend's social media if they've been passed away for a good amount of time. It's just what happens, but for now Kirsty is still on social media.

Not long before Kirsty's funeral (I still vigorously dislike that word), I had been to a publishing conference in Leicester. I found it difficult to concentrate but it was nice to meet Sophie Hannah (the author that has taken on the Agatha Christie reboot of novels). When I got back to Raunds (Ellen had been looking after Sabat for the day), I was surprised to see a letter from Legal & General for Kirsty. Her parents had opened it and said I'd better sit down as they had some news for me. They then handed me the letter.

The contents went thus. Kirsty had missed a payment on her life insurance policy and if the payment wasn't made to bring it up to date, then the policy would become null and void. The policy was for £100,000 in the event of death. This came as a complete shock. I had no idea she had a life insurance policy. And now what was I supposed to do? Did I lose a wife and gain not only a dog, but £100,000 as well? This felt so wrong.

I drove home in a stunned, confused silence. Since the day she had died every day would throw up some new shock, some new punch that kept me down. This was where Sabat was an absolute star.

Each day I'd wake up and he'd be on the sofa downstairs. Our relationship was so different from the one he'd had with Kirsty. She would go downstairs and he'd go nuts, like she'd been gone for weeks. He'd jump up, make funny noises and his tail would wag like a helicopter. He'd usually demand belly rubs then offer his butt to be rubbed too.

I'd go in the living room and he'd look at me, tail gently wagging and we'd say 'hello'. It was like he'd won second prize and only because third prize wasn't available. It wasn't that I didn't feel his love; I did. But I wasn't the mummy who had saved him. I wasn't Kirsty. When we went for a walk, he'd still be the same, pulling like mad for the first half a mile then he'd settle into his rhythm and stop being a dickhead. The one thing he was very good at was doing absolutely daft things. His ability to make me laugh was astonishing. And every time he did, he helped me through the sadness.

One night, I'm not sure when, but it was in the first three months when it was just him and me, I was woken early in the morning by rain lashing the windows and lightning flashing in the sky. There was a huge clap of thunder and I was aware that Sabat was by the bed. When Kirsty was alive, we always closed the bedroom door and Sabat slept on the sofa downstairs. He had his bed in the living room, but he rarely went in it and it didn't bother me. Now it was just us, I wanted him to know he could see me if he wanted to. In those early days, I'd often wake to see a wet, black nose near my head. It was like Sabat was checking to see if I'd lived through the night. But this was different. I could see that he was scared. I stroked his head; told him everything was ok and invited him onto the bed. He jumped up and I stroked him and talked to him calmly and told him he was safe. My words and my manner had an effect and he calmed down and fell asleep near me. I fell asleep too and when I woke up at the normal waking time, Sabat was gone. Back to his place on the sofa and when I went downstairs, his tail wagged a little more and he invited me to rub his belly. That was the first time I felt I'd done something right by him. He knew I was there for him.

The next development came in June. The year before I had secured tickets for ABBA Voyage, the hologram show that is still playing in London. I've seen it twice and each time it has amazed me. The first time I went with a fellow ABBA fan and we were in the 'dance area'. A clever piece of marketing which meant 'standing area'. It did afford a close-up view of the ABBAtars though and it was incredible. I kept looking and I couldn't tell the difference between what I was seeing and a real person. All of which meant the show was brilliant and I knew then that Kirsty would have hated it. Not the show itself, but her PTSD would have meant she couldn't enjoy being that close to people for two hours. A little sign that my life had moved on in a different way.

However, a day in London also gave me something else. Covid. It was the first time I'd had it and although it wasn't awful, it stopped my training in its tracks. Which led to a major change in our routine. As I couldn't run, I started walking Sabat twice a day and that included every evening. I realised very quickly that not doing this before was really dumb. By letting him walk, sniff and pee he was getting his evening fix of doggy dopamine and meant his bladder was empty when he went to sleep. Why had I never thought of this before and why hadn't Kirsty and I gone on evening walks every night? Hindsight wins again.

Chapter 17
Illegal & Immoral

The life insurance policy. What had seemed a ray of light soon became a yoke around my neck. The next day I remembered that Kirsty had mentioned her policy and we had even discussed it with an insurance broker back in the winter of 2021 and then I'd promptly forgotten about it. Initially I contacted Legal & General and told them that Kirsty had passed away. They made all the right noises, directed me to the claims department who then sent me a batch of forms. I waited until the funeral was out of the way before dealing with them. £100,000 was a lot of money to me and I thought it would help to offset the chaos of her death and my contribution towards the funeral. What I didn't want to do was fill in the forms incorrectly and jeopardise the claim. This was all new to me; the only thing I'd ever claimed for was a car accident.

I sought advice from my stepdad, who had worked in the industry for a long time, filled in the forms and then waited. They came back to me quite quickly and explained that as Kirsty had been subjected to an autopsy and we didn't have the results back yet they couldn't settle until a formal cause of death had been declared. Plus, there was the inquest to be settled as well. In the summer of 2022, this all felt like a long way off.

It felt like they were on my side: the bereaved widower. They were always polite, they sounded sympathetic and helpful. As the months went by, I found that wasn't the case at all. I stopped calling them Legal & General and instead called them Illegal & Immoral.

I could have written a book just on the fight to get the claim sorted, but you deserve better and so did I, so this is a summation of what happened.

They turned down the claim based on the original sign-up form and the details disclosed at the time and the thing they kept on about was that Kirsty had claimed to be a non-smoker at the time she took out the policy. Her medical records showed otherwise. Their access to Kirsty's medical records and my lack of access to them became a constant source of frustration. This seemed absurd as smoking had nothing to do with her death. To me it was irrelevant.

Kirsty had led a difficult life in the years before we were reunited. Her ability to choose abusive partners was uncanny. The past three had all beaten her and eroded her confidence. The one who broke her arm that would lead to the Complex Regional Pain Syndrome was the worst of the lot and she had been with him for nearly five years. (He was later convicted in court. He got eight months of community service. And people wonder why women are reluctant to press charges. To be fair, in this case, even the police were disgusted by this sentence.)

This led to bouts of depression, PTSD, as well as frequent trips to the hospital. In one year, she was in the A & E department eighteen times. All of this was in her medical records and Illegal & Immoral seemed to be allowed far too much access as far as I was concerned.

The case dragged on for six months before they turned down the claim, long before the inquest and final cause of death. Nothing was ever made about the salesman who had sold her the policy and how he recorded Kirsty's answers. I felt all along that they had taken advantage of a fragile woman's nature and were interested only in the commission that he made on the sale of the policy. The way they treated me eroded my mental health to the point that when I got the final verdict, I was questioning my time on the planet.

I am a robust person. I can cope with anything that is thrown at me, but that battle with the insurance company affected me deeply. One morning in October I was running with Sabat and began to wonder if life was just all too much. I had my son, I had friends and people who relied on me. But when we got home and I sat sweating and looked at Sabat's brown eyes I knew I had a new purpose. To give this dog who had come from a kill shelter to England to meet a woman who loved him with all her heart and had then left him with another person, I would make sure he had the best life a dog could have. Love would help us through all the shit we'd have to deal with even if right now I didn't know how.

Before we leave the subject of life insurance, let me say this. I researched Legal & General and found that they have a policy of rejecting 17% of all claims made to them. Life insurance, pet insurance, car insurance and home insurance. They will look for every way they can turn down your claim. If your toddler destroys your TV that's one thing; but if they're turning down a life insurance claim, that's a whole new level of evil.

And to the question many of you will have wanted to ask. How did Kirsty die? Lots of people ask me and this is the answer I give: Complications relating to the cocktail of drugs that she was taking for her medical conditions. At the inquest with the Northampton Coroner in April 2023 the verdict reached was an open verdict. In short, this means that it is somewhat of a mystery as to how she died.

Here's something else that people need to understand. We are by nature, curious creatures. When people die young, whether famous, infamous or what we'd call normal, we want to know how it could happen, but please think of their loved ones left behind. They don't want to experience those feelings of pain any more frequently than they must, so if they don't want to disclose the reason for the person's death, respect their wishes. It is a private matter and they have no obligation to tell the casual observer, no matter how well-meaning. Taylor Hawkins of the Foo Fighters died four days after Kirsty and his exact cause of death has never been revealed. Sometimes it's only for the family to know.

Life wasn't all completely awful. In the summer of 2022 I entered the National Entrepreneur of the Year Awards and although I didn't win the category I did enter, I won an award I didn't know I had been entered for.

I have been a member of the Entrepreneurs Circle since September 2011. It has taught me so much about business and I get constant support from them. They were lovely when we got married and they were wonderful in their help and support after she died.

In July 2021, I was asked to run one of the local meetings that they were instigating across the UK. For Kirsty and me it was something that we ran together. I ran the meeting, she helped set up the room, charmed the members and took lots of photographs. We were a great team.

After her death, the meetings continued and we still talk about her three years on. The award I won was for Ambassador (that's what they call the folks who run the local meetings) of the Year. As a national award I was extremely proud of this; even more so as it had been voted for by local members and at EC HQ. As my name was read out, I was shocked, but proud. I collected my award from Jimmy Carr, the comedian. For someone with such a sharp wit, he couldn't have been more lovely. He spoke to me on stage and later when I got my photo taken with him. Jimmy, if you ever read this, you're a top guy. It was he who pointed out that almost everyone in the audience was on their feet. It was the highlight of 2022. Not that there was much else to celebrate.

Part Four

Phoenix

Chapter 18
Future Planning

2022 was brutal. There's no other way to look at it. In August of that year another close friend passed away suddenly. Jeff Gonsalves had trained in martial arts with me for almost twenty years. I remember the first time I ever met him and he would be at almost every seminar I ever hosted. He was the sweetest man. One night I messaged him and he replied, 'On the way back from Thailand. Talk in the morning.' I was stunned to receive a phone call twelve hours later from one of Jeff's students saying that Jeff had passed away. My brain couldn't compute. But I was waiting for a call from Jeff. How could he no longer be here? Shortly after, I learned that he had died in his kitchen in front of his wife, Vickie. They had returned from a dream holiday, Jeff had run a bath after feeling grubby following the long flight and died as the result of blood clots in his lungs. He dropped dead in front of her. Can you imagine anything worse?

I was stunned. I now knew how the world felt when they heard of Kirsty's death. It was all too incredible for words. Is sudden death worse than the death you prepare for? I don't know, neither are any fun. It just seems to me that sudden death is like a car crash. Hard to comprehend and difficult to recover from. I did all I could to help Vickie in terms of words of support, but I know she misses Jeff as much now as she did three years ago.

His funeral was well attended although it was disappointing that someone scheduled to deliver words for him didn't show up. A cousin stepped in and was brilliant. The vicar that day also spent far too long promoting his church and not talking about Jeff. I wanted to shake him.

Let's talk about funerals. I mentioned one earlier that I went to where a man seemed to have had no life, he just existed. Is that how you see your life? I've been to burials and cremations; I've been to green funerals and interesting funerals. However, most don't have enough thought put into them. Unlike weddings, you only ever get one shot at the funeral. If you were close to the person that died, attend the event. You owe them that.

Think about your funeral and who you really want there. Think about the music you want. Plan it. Tell someone that they are in charge of it and make sure you can trust them. Pay for it before it happens; there are all sorts of funeral plans for that. Don't be a burden, be an inspiration. None of us know when our time is up. Kirsty and Jeff were sudden. My great friend and teacher, Richard Bustillo was gone in six days. Others suffer cancer or dementia or some other awful disease. Just make plans. Accepting you'll die gives you the freedom to live.

Also, make provisions for your pets. With Sabat he could have gone with me or Kirsty's parents. He was set no matter where he went, because we love him. Other dogs are not so lucky and they lose not only their owner, but also their home. I've met many rescue dogs who experienced this. Imagine the confusion and sadness these poor animals go through. It's bloody awful.

If you're the sort of person who thinks they can't face these conversations, it's time to grow up and accept your responsibility. You make plans to make life better. Make plans for death to make those who love you have their life better. I will never forget sitting in that funeral directors choosing the funeral we wanted for Kirsty, the car, the coffin and later the flowers. Then we had to find a celebrant, choose the music and the theme. It was terrible. Don't put your parents or children through that level of agony. They will be coping with enough, just grieving you.

There were some highlights and some weird things that happened too. The last film that Kirsty and I went to see was 'Phantom of the Open'. We saw it the Saturday before Kirsty died and we enjoyed it. During the trailers there was one for Baz Luhrman's 'Elvis', starring Austin Butler. We were far more excited about this.

The film wasn't released until June and I went to see it five times at the cinema with three different people. On the day it was released I saw the afternoon premier and then went to a different cinema with a friend and watched it again the same day. I absolutely loved the film and so wished I could have seen it with Kirsty.

The first cinema experience we ever had together was to see the 1970 Elvis documentary 'That's The Way It Is.' So much of our life revolved around him. After the first time I saw 'Elvis', I chastised Kirsty on the way home. 'You would have bloody loved it,' I said. There was no reply. Later in the year when it hit the streaming services I paid for the film and watched it another five times. Perhaps it was another form of release.

One of the strange things that happened was when I went to the cinema for the first time without her. I went to see the World War II film, 'Operation Mincemeat.' I went to the same cinema we'd been to that last time and was rather surprised when I found myself in exactly the same seat in the same theatre as I had been with Kirsty a couple of months before. Her seat remained empty. And they were still showing the 'Elvis' trailer.

A while later, I went to see 'A Man Called Otto'. I thought it was a comedy, not a black comedy and philosophical piece about a man whose wife has died and he has decided to commit suicide. I nearly walked out. And to add to the synchronicity, Tom Hanks played Colonel Tom Parker in 'Elvis' and now here he was playing 'Otto'. I know it can be seen as coincidence, but these things kept happening.

In August I went to the Entrepreneurs Circle offices when Nigel Botterill generously gave me an hour's coaching on how to get my business back on track. I had asked if it was okay to take Sabat with me and they allowed me to. Lots of people went nuts over Sabat and he loved the fuss. Someone asked if he could have some chicken. I said yes. After a successful trip I went back home, dropped Sabat off and went to teach that night. I wasn't prepared for what greeted me when I walked in. The chicken had not agreed with Sabat at all. The poor pup had left two piles of very sloppy dog poo in the living room and my office. This was a new one for me.

He looked so sheepish and thought he was going to get a terrible telling off. I knew it wasn't his fault, so let him out into the garden, reassured him and let him recover there.

Meanwhile, I got to work. I phoned Caroline and told her what had happened and she gave me some great advice. With diarrhoea or sloppy dog poo, don't try and scoop it up with bundles of kitchen roll. Find a flat knife and scoop it onto the blade then pour it onto the kitchen roll. This stops the brown stuff mixing in the carpet. This was genius. I did throw the knife away after. I wouldn't recommend Russian Roulette with the knife in the drawer no matter how well you clean it. The two lots took me the best part of an hour to clean up and Sabat seemed much better knowing he wasn't in trouble and that the house didn't smell of dog shit. Bicarbonate of soda is a wonderful thing.

The following morning, he'd had another accident on a rug this time and it was much easier to clean. And that has been the only occasion that has happened. He's such a brilliant dog. If he needs the toilet he always goes outside.

A few weeks later I was invited back to EC HQ for an interview for a project they were putting together and thought I might be a suitable candidate. I was interviewed by four people and although I felt I did well in the earlier rounds I fluffed the last one. This has been my only job interview in thirty-two years and now I'm glad I didn't get it. It has allowed me to flourish and grow at the best pace for me to fully recover. In September 2022, I was definitely not healed. It was the day that Queen Elizabeth died, so my interview very quickly became insignificant.

Chapter 19
Grey Cells

There had been some signs that my brain was starting to work again. I rewrote the martial arts syllabus to help retain more students and to build the business and I had the logo redesigned. Both of these would prove to work out well over the next three years. I came to the realisation that I had to let the fight go for the insurance money and concentrate on doing everything that was best for myself and Sabat.

It was amazing how quickly things started to change once I let go of the negativity and embraced the future. The very first thing that happened was when I was teaching one Thursday evening. We play music during the classes and a late 90s one hit wonder came up on the playlist. It's a great song, but one line caught my attention. It said, very succinctly, that there was a purpose to living and not giving up. A solid beat, a beautifully written line delivered with passion. It stopped me in my tracks and I played the song again. I left the class that night in a very good mood.

I remembered the song from when it first came out in 1998, but the reason it stuck in my mind was its inclusion in a talk I saw by a lady called Debra Searle. She had spoken at the Entrepreneurs Circle Conference in 2014 and was by far the best speaker, in a lineup that included Steve Wozniak, the co-founder of Apple. Her story was of how she had rowed across the Atlantic in 2002. It had started as a race with her husband also in the boat, but they discovered he had a fear of open water. While they were at sea! He was lifted off the boat after two weeks and she carried on, finally completing the 3,300 miles after three months. Her tale was brilliantly told and I watched the recording of it again the day after hearing the song.

I started to feel the old energy come back to me. An energy I hadn't felt for six months. I had been forcing myself through the days, but now it was time to move forward. Kirsty never left my thoughts, but there was no going back. I began my plan.

Almost immediately a lady contacted me out of the blue and told me about her business and how she helped those who have been struggling with grief. I think she heard about me through the EC. We talked for a while, I told her my story and she said she would send me a package. It was amazing. There were some lovely tea lights and a couple of books, but the highlight was a leather-bound journal. Every page pristine and waiting for me to write down my thoughts.

On the first page I wrote:

'Journal begins. 22.10.22.

The future is hidden in these pages.

The results are for the world to see. The journey is mine to walk/run/drive.'

At the bottom of the page, I added a quote on 26th November. It was from the singer, Beverley Craven.

"It's hunger, not satisfaction, that drives ambition."

I still have that journal and use it from time to time.

I wrote down the things I wanted to do, the places I want to go, the car I want to drive and where I wanted to live. I also wrote down all the things I would do to achieve my ambitions. It was simple to me. Serve more people and earn the means to live the life I craved.

However, there was a problem to overcome. I was very aware of how quickly my energy still dissipated. Every day I would take Sabat out for two miles, come home, have breakfast and almost always fall asleep for thirty minutes or more. I had to get past this sleep apnoea. That would come in time.

If journaling was the first thing, then music came next. If one song could have a dramatic effect, what about a playlist that would raise my spirits every time I heard it? I began the task. Within a day or so I had more than sixty songs to listen to. Now it was time to dreamboard.

I'm a visual kind of guy. I like to look at stuff. Pictures, photos, videos and films. I've had dreamboards for over twenty years. Some things happen, some things don't but they help to keep me on track, when my wife doesn't die along with good friends and Covid doesn't close me down. I was aware that I would need two dreamboards. One for the coming year and another for ten years. My previous ten-year dreamboard was out of date and I was going to update it with Kirsty; now that option no longer existed, I needed a new plan. I called it 'no wife, new life.'

In my journal I continued writing down all the places I wanted to go and the things I wanted to experience. I costed it all. I wrote down which goals would be achieved soon and which would come later. I put as much detail into it as possible. I wanted to step into this new life and Sabat was going to do as much of it as he could.

I went to a local stationers and got a new cork board for the one-year version and a larger piece of card for the ten-year version. Next, I went on the internet and found all the pictures I would need. I felt like I was six years old and was in an art class at school. None of that mattered. What did matter was that I could see my future and compared to the despair of crying and grieving this was incredible. I knew there was life again.

It took about three weeks to complete, stopping at times to teach and work on the business. When the dreamboards were done, I put one on the far wall and one closer to me. I could see both, every day. I had something to live for and Sabat was going to be my lucky charm.

Chapter 20
Anniversaries

Birthdays, Christmas, wedding days, in fact any anniversary brings tougher days, but it is the first of each of these that raises the emotions the most. For me, the first one was the first anniversary and the trip to Hartfield. Next up was Kirsty's birthday. That was 14th June and I was going to spread the rest of her ashes on this day. The site I had chosen was overlooking the dog field at Priors Hall Park that she used to walk Sabat every day. That would give her a good view of all the other dogs running around there and we could visit regularly.

Two of her dog walking friends came to watch (Brian and Rita Little) and her mum, Ellen, came over as well. At 7.30am on what would have been Kirsty's 42nd birthday, I let her ashes drift over the hedgerow. Like in Hartfield, I was surprised at how much was visible when it all settled. Over the following weeks, I would watch as the green would reappear in the leaves and the grey fell into the ground below. For a long time, I thought I should organise some permanent memorial to her memory, but so far that hasn't happened. Sabat and I still visit on a regular basis.

On Kirsty's birthday in 2025, Sabat and I visited to wish her fond greetings and we bumped into Brian and Rita again. They have remained friends throughout. The most curious thing about this meeting was that Sabat and I were out running and had set off ninety minutes later than originally scheduled, so we had no right to run into Brian and Rita at all that day. But they were also standing in exactly the same place as they had when I spread Kirsty's ashes in 2022. Was my ghostly wife bringing us together again? You'll make your own judgement.

The same day was also the first time I ever read any of these stories in public. The Force was strong that day.

The first Christmas was a curious affair. The people of Priors Hall Park (that's a developing village outside of Corby, Northamptonshire) like their Christmas lights. Some people put them up as soon as the Halloween decorations come down. Normally I think that's too early, but in 2022, it helped me massively. Every evening Sabat and I would set out to walk or run and the lights made me feel good inside. It would be my first Christmas without Kirsty, but I'd only had two with her. Sabat also came up with one of his party tricks on Christmas Day.

Sabat loves chasing rabbits. Fortunately, he is usually too slow to react or to catch the cotton tails. Except on Christmas Day 2022. It hadn't taken long to meet other dog owners as Sabat is such a sociable dog. That meant that he quickly grew his pack: Tilly the Beagle. Dexter the Beagle. Molly the Spaniel and others such as Rocky the Cocker Spaniel and Gibbs the Weimaraner. I was also learning the owners names, but that always came after. The dogs were first. So the owners were Debbie, Steve, Lucia and Alexandra and Sue and Jez.

We arranged to meet up on Christmas morning and walked in the local valley. We were on old groundworks for British Steel. We'd walk to the end of the valley and then back. Most of the dogs were off lead and happy to play together. Sabat disappeared for a few minutes and then reappeared with something in his mouth. At first I couldn't see what it was, then I realised.

It was a rabbit. I tried to get it off him, but he ran into one of the small ponds and all I could hear was the water splashing and the crunch of bones. I called him again and he ran to another pond and continued with his breakfast. He reappeared and dropped the carcass by the pond. He had chewed it's head off. He was so pleased with himself.

I thought it best that I removed it from the valley and went to throw it over a fence. It felt inordinately heavy and as I looked down, I saw that Rocky had his teeth clamped around the rabbit's legs! I managed to get him off and the poor headless rabbit sailed through the air. Dogs may look cute and fluffy, but all of them have the potential to be a killer.

It was the most memorable Christmas Day walk I've ever been on. I also wondered how he had caught it. Was it already dead and he picked it up or had he caught it on the run? As he never had before and never has since, I wondered if Kirsty had tripped the poor bunny as a Christmas treat for him.

Since those days the original pack has become somewhat dissolved and his friends these days are Bodie the Labrador, Booma (I think he's a bear, but he's maybe a large German Shepherd) and Scout, the wiry rescue with a fascination for chasing tennis balls. The owners, Karl and Sarah (not a couple), are our regular Sunday morning companions. Sabat loves seeing his friends.

I turned sixty in February 2023 and Sabat made sure it was a memorable day. It began with a normal walk in the valley with the dogs Tilly and Gibbs. All was well until our return in the valley. Sabat and Gibbs decided to climb the cliff face and walk along the top of the cliffs. Tilly followed them. I followed them too, worried that they would try and jump off. It turned out that they were far smarter than me. While I trawled through wet grass, they ran along nimble footed until we got near the end and the descent. Sabat and Gibbs got down easily, but we had to convince Tilly not to jump off the cliff into the valley. Sabat went back to guide her down. I just wanted breakfast!

The first anniversary of Kirsty's passing was horrible, but I found the lead up to the day worse. It was like following a disaster on the news and then seeing it happen. Of each subsequent anniversary none have been as bad as the first. I would expect most people who have been through grief to experience the same.

The only other significant anniversary was the second birthday of Kirsty's since she'd passed. During a walk in the valley with Tilly and Gibbs again, a woman accused Sabat of trying to attack her. He did nothing of the sort, he just walked up to her to say 'hello'. I pointed that out to her, but she was having none of it and started shouting at me. I guess Kirsty's birthday affected me more than I realised because I totally lost my temper. We got into a shouting match and I totally over-reacted. Later I felt embarrassed and it's never happened since. All of us have moments of loss of control. Fortunately, no further action was taken. I kept a closer eye on Sabat after that.

In time I learned that most dog owners are nice people, but there are always some that don't understand the maxim of 'Don't be a dick.' So far, we have navigated the choppy waters of dog ownership.

All I would add is to expect anniversaries to be difficult and be aware of your mood swings on such days. I have found that the sharpness of your mood decreases over time, but that might just be me.

Chapter 21
Dog Life

Writing these stories has reminded me how little I knew about dogs before Sabat became my sole responsibility. The following may be obvious to many of you, but these are my observations as a novice.

Let's address 'on the lead' versus 'off the lead', because it seems to me that most people fall into either camp. On our walk last night, we met Sabat's white Staffie friend, George. George is an off the lead dog. His owner walks around the village with this lovely, happy dog all the time. Some on the lead folks would have a fit at seeing this powerful dog waddling along. Sabat sussed him from the start though. He was on the lead when we first met George at the park. I let him off and the two of them played for about twenty minutes, no problems.

I know of other dogs that have been attacked in similar circumstances. When I first had Sabat, I'd walk him as Kirsty had. On the lead on the paths, off the lead on the grass. If she called him, he would come. I didn't realise at first that Sabat is not a disobedient dog; he is an alpha dog though. He was testing his boundaries continually and that all came to a head when he escaped on the main road. I was so lucky I didn't lose him that day. He was leading me, not the other way around.

When the valley opened, that helped a lot. It gave the chance to assert control over Sabat, but it took a long time and he was worse if he was with his pack.

Now I walk him on the lead most of the time. I let him off when it is safe to do so and put him back on if I see another dog on the lead. It works most of the time. Likewise, if there is another dog roaming freely, I will usually let Sabat off the lead to play. It's a case of paying attention to the circumstances, the other dog and watching the owners. There are a lot of very nervous owners out there and that means nervous dogs. Avoid as much aggravation as you can, by thinking about other dogs, rather than just yours.

What about the lead you use? Kirsty experimented with all different types. A halti worked very well, but Sabat hated it. Kirsty tried him with a harness for a while; that was ok, but as he got stronger the harness worked in his favour. He was like a carthorse pulling a wagon. She finally settled on a choke collar combined with a variable length lead. She would attach this to a harness clipped to her waist. I would use the same combination for running Sabat. When she died, I carried on using the harness for running and walked him with the lead. It's all worked well.

Best poo bags? My favourites are from Pets At Home. A decent thickness (less digits in the poo) and nice colours so easy to see.

What do you feed your dog? At first, I gave him the packet meals that Kirsty had been serving him. That went on for a while thanks to the voucher that the dog walkers got for me. I remembered that sometimes Kirsty would feed him on raw food, so I thought I'd try that. He loved it and he's been on it ever since. I mix it with some biscuits and he's a happy pup. Sometimes I'll change that up with a can of tuna instead. He likes that too.

Which is what led to him changing my life. A year or so after it had just been us, I started to wonder if some better quality protein might be good for my overall health, and for building strength when weight training.

I had been vegetarian for 22 years at this point. I tried a tuna salad and Sabat was baffled. He'd never seen a human eat his food before. As for me, no ill effects. The next progression was to fish and chips. I was surprised how much the piece of cod satisfied my hunger and that was with giving Sabat a third of the fish. He still came around begging for more.

I read Chris Van Teleken's book 'Ultra Processed People'. I was transformed. The final convincer was the gym owner and influencer, Eddie Abbew. He's a real character and goes into supermarkets, picking up all sorts of convenience food and declaring it as 'sugary shit'.

That convinced me to try steak for the first time. I wondered if there would be any aftereffects, but was pleased to say that there were none. And Sabat was very impressed. At first, I bought all my meat from the same farm shop that I now bought all my fruit and veg, until I found D & L Hadden's Butchers in Corby Old Village. When I told the owner, Davey, that I used to be vegetarian he began to educate me in the ways of meat.

This meant sausages, bacon and black pudding. Then Scotch pies and square sausage. The effect was unexpected. I got stronger and every week in the gym I could feel improvements. I won't be going back to the ultra-processed vegetarian 'food' again. Sabat couldn't be happier.

If we're really hungry, occasionally we'll eat a vegan.

I read once 'A dog's life is reflected in the experiences that they have'. That made me think and think a lot. It seems to me that Covid was a significant event in pet ownership. With people locked down, more people wanted pets of all kinds, but especially dogs. A lot of those dog owners were like me: inexperienced and didn't know what they were doing. Many have done well, some have done fine and some should never be near any kind of pet. It has led to all sorts of issues with rehoming dogs. Can you imagine that of a human? For six months you settle into a home environment and then suddenly you're put in a shelter or worse, abandoned on the streets. Dogs are loyal, loving creatures. Imagine the trauma a dog goes through when they are left to their own devices without the home they have grown used to.

I know that in some cases this is a blessing. In which case, anyone who harms an animal goes to the top of my shit list. I can't bear the thought of a dog being mistreated. How a person treats an animal, is how they treat the world.

That being said I try to include Sabat in as many experiences as I can. I've just discovered he can go in The Range, so we went shopping and he went in a lift for the first time. He wasn't sure about that at all, but he behaved impeccably. During the promotion for this book, I took him networking. He hadn't done that before either and the people there were a bit shocked too. However, Sabat is a relaxed, chilled dog and he was great with everyone.

The only time he's been on holiday was the Weymouth trip that Kirsty and I took him on so he's overdue another one. Dogs are more accepted in public places now which makes things easier and I'm more confident about taking him to places. That is the nature of dog ownership. They reflect you. When Kirsty was here, Sabat was more excitable, and was a very Zebedee type dog. Obviously he's older now, but we lead a calm life, despite all the stresses we've been through. That reflects upon his behaviour.

Earlier in the book, I mentioned that he didn't play with any toys for about a year after Kirsty died. He had lost the joy of life. I'm happy to report that isn't the case now and we frequently have play sessions.

He's also a constant source of inspiration for improving my business. I have to work to provide for Sabat and for me. I can't let him down. The dog is a survivor. He survived weeks on the streets of Bucharest, he survived the loss of his true love and we have survived everything that has happened together.

Dog life is a good life.

Chapter 22
Sausages

I moved to Priors Hall Park, by lucky circumstances. I had never heard of the place in 2011 and was introduced to it by a letting agent. Back then they had the daft idea of calling it 'Londonshire' to attract those with apartments that sold for a million pounds and would find a one-hour commute on a train enjoyable. The first houses were built to model the same look as Marylebone and Baker Street; presumably without a wailing saxophone in the background.

I was shown to a C-shaped terrace of stone cottages and had the choice of two. I looked at both and chose the one I liked most. I lived there for three years until moving to a larger house 400m away with the intention of moving in with a lady and her two children. We were in a relationship; not just a random person I'd met in a queue for some stamps. However, the relationship didn't work as planned and for a long time it was me, my books and music. Until Kirsty appeared in 2020. At first it was just a Saturday, then quickly it became Saturday and Sunday, then Friday night too. At Christmas 2020, she moved in for ten days, went home to her parent's house for two days then moved back in as lockdown number three kicked in. She was there until her dying day. Her last breath taken in the bedroom on the top floor.

Six months after she passed, I got a letter from the landlord asking me to leave. I negotiated to pay a higher rent and they let me stay. At the time, I couldn't believe that they had acted so callously. To me, this was the place that had been my home for almost ten years and where my wife had died. To them, they just wanted more rent. I attached the meaning to the house;

they attached profit and loss. It helped me cut the emotional strings.

A year later they came back with the same thing. This time I didn't fight. I was just pissed off. It took months to find another place, but find it I did. Only one mile away, in a village location with amazing views and a church 200m away and the river 50m away. It was perfect. Much smaller though and I had gathered a lot of stuff in ten years.

Not just my personal things, but when 3P closed down everything went in the garage. There was very little that needed keeping so it was time to clear out. And, of course, all the things of Kirsty's that I hadn't thrown away up until now. It was time to be ruthless. I was glad that I had waited as well. Now I had the emotional bandwidth to cope with the decisions that had to be made.

I found all sorts of things that Kirsty had hidden deep in the garage and in nooks and crannies throughout the house. I found hundreds of photographs, from Kirsty's early life and her family. I found her passport which had stubbornly stayed hidden until then. But most surprisingly, I also found keepsakes from the abusive relationships she had been in. It made no sense to me. Why would you keep things from people who hurt you? These men had broken her bones, sliced her arm open with a broken plate and left scars on her face, as well as her soul.

I found letters she had kept from these monsters, where they declared their love, despite putting her in hospital multiple times. I decided it was time these 'keepsakes' were no longer kept. She deserved better.

I took them into the garden and placed them all in a small wooden box. Then I set fire to them. Their control gone in this life and the next. It all burned well, the box along with it all. Until it came to the time when I put out the flames. I was about to go into the kitchen to get some water, then I had a better idea. I would put it out. Looking around, no one could see into the garden so I pulled out the fire hose (a very small hose it must be said) and a yellow stream disappeared into the flames making the evil hiss and the false promises bubble. The fire died down and all that was left was ash. I let it dry in the wind and swept it into the bin when it had.

Moving day arrived and I had asked for volunteers to help. The response was amazing. Fourteen people turned up. With some co-ordination we moved an entire 4-bedroom house in ninety minutes. My new neighbours must have thought the Jehovah's Witnesses had turned up.

As a way of thanking everyone I took them to the breakfast place across the road. We all piled in and had a great time with the bacon, eggs and Sabat's favourite: the sausages.

When we left, I had to do some things in Kettering then returned home. It was now 1.30pm. After about ten minutes I realised that Sabat wasn't around. I checked the garden and, to my horror, realised the back gate hadn't been closed properly. Panicking, I ran out of the gate and a young couple asked if I was looking for a dog. Everyone knows the looking for a dog look! I said 'yes' and they pointed me in the direction he had gone.

Right towards the main road through Weldon! A busy road. I looked up and down and couldn't see him. Then I wondered. Had he gone back to the breakfast place? I ran to the rear entrance as the shop was now closed.

And I heard the words 'Your dog is in the kitchen!'

I had lived in Weldon for three hours and people already knew who we were!

Leaving that house gave me all sorts of emotions. First of all, I had lived there for ten years and it was a nice house. I could spread out. One bedroom was converted to a library with 2000 books in it. Another was my office and yet another stored my music collection. It was also, of course, where my worst day happened. The house was packed with Kirsty memories, but the truth was I had the memories. Bricks and mortar remembered nothing. It provided the vehicle for me to make those memories.

Once the house was empty, I cleaned it all top to bottom, which some much appreciated help and by 9pm on the hottest day of the year, I closed the door, locked it and dropped the keys off. My time there was over. It was time to make new memories.

Chapter 23
My hero

It began with a text when I woke up. Actually the text had been sent in the early hours, but I turn my phone off every night and it pinged when the phone went back on. It was from my friend, Sue. 'Rosie has gone missing. It has been 36 hours and not a peep. She escaped from my mum's house. I'm so upset and I can't sleep.' Sent at 2.13am.

I immediately replied, offering our help. I had a feeling that Sabat might be useful. For four hours there was no reply, then suddenly the phone sparked into life. Sue was in a village, near Kettering, looking for Rosie.

'I'm in Loddington looking. She was seen at a bus stop at 8am this morning, when approached, she ran away.'

I thought this odd, because I was sure that Rosie didn't carry cash or a debit card, so why wait for a bus? I offered my help again and the reply I got was:

'It's like a needle in a haystack. It's vast out here, she could be anywhere. I've been wandering the streets, calling her name. Nothing.'

I said that we'd be over straightaway. I gathered Sabat's treat box, a bottle of water, a bowl and some poo bags. Off we went. It only took twenty-five minutes to get to Loddington and another five to find Sue. She was outside a field on the road out of Loddington to Harringworth. She was on the phone when we arrived. Sabat is normally excited to see Sue, but this time he could feel that something wasn't right. She was on the phone to the drone operator. Who knew there were drone operators to find lost dogs?

When she came off the phone Sue explained that dogs usually search in triangles, so if they get lost, they keep going around in geometric shapes until they get home. Which might be ok for a dog the size of Sabat, but Rosie is a grey Shih Tzu and weighs 7kg. Not a dog for the outdoors. Who had by now been roaming around for 44 hours.

The one piece of hope was the sighting in Loddington by the bus stop. She'd obviously thought this was a good place to shelter. The weather had been kind as well with dry and warm conditions. Not hot, but enough to keep the little dog dry at least.

I suggested we leave where we were and head back into Loddington. Sue agreed. By now, stress had almost stopped her from making decisions.

We got to the bus stop which had a short road and housing estate, just behind it. We parked there and I walked Sabat around to the bus stop. He sniffed all over. If he knew something, he couldn't tell us, but he did pull us in the direction of the Cransley Road. That's where Rosie had come from in the first place. Maybe Sabat was telling us something.

We came upon two fields, which we had a quick look in, but my brain was telling me that we should head towards Cransley. Within minutes everything changed.

Sue and I were only on the road sixty seconds and a car pulled up. 'Are you looking for a dog?' See, I told you that we have a look. 'We've just seen a grey dog running down the road.'

It had to be Rosie, but was it possible that we had found her so easily?

'You get in the car with them,' I said. 'We'll follow on behind.'

The moment that Sue was in the car with the random couple, Sabat was pulling. He knew something was down this road. We set off running, the afternoon sun starting to shine through. After two minutes the car returned with Sue, but no Rosie.

‘Go and get your car and follow me,’ I told Sue. The car sped off while Sabat and I continued to jog down the hill. At the bottom of Cransley Road there is a crossing over a stream and to the right an area of undergrowth. Sabat was sniffing and checking everywhere. Has hard as I looked, I couldn’t see anything moving, but by the way that Sabat was acting I was sure that something lurked in the foliage. After a couple of minutes, we continued up the hill towards Cransley, but we’d only gone 100m when a car tooted its horn from behind us. I stopped running and turned around. A car had stopped and right in front of it, running like a mop head fuelled by nitrous was a little grey dog.

‘Rosie!’ I hollered.

For a moment, she stopped and looked at me. And ran off in the opposite direction. I called again, but it made no difference. Rosie was heading away and running much faster than I realised a Shih Tzu could run. Sabat and I took after her, except now there was a car behind me, so I was running down the road, Sabat leading the way and me with hand outstretched stopping the car from getting past me. We ran on. As we passed the area of undergrowth and headed the way we had come, I saw Sue’s car. And Sue saw Rosie.

She stopped and jumped out of the car. Rosie looked at her and continued running. Then stopped. She must have thought, ‘Hey, that’s my mum.’ She ran to Sue and by now I was a few feet away. I waved the cars on and checked to make sure nothing was coming up from behind. For at least two minutes, dog and owner cried, shook and hugged. Rosie was grubby and matted from her two-day adventure, but most importantly, she was now safe.

Sabat jumped in the back of Sue’s car, she got in the passenger seat and I drove back to where we had left my car.

When I stopped, we all got out and I poured water into the bowl. Rosie lapped at it, tiny tongue flickering pink. I opened the treat box and Rosie ate everything offered. Sabat got some too.

Sue was still shaking as was Rosie. An old couple came out to talk to us and told us how they had tried to catch Rosie, but she was too scared and too fast. Everyone was relieved that dog and owner were back together.

If I could have given Sabat a medal there and then I would have. For 44 hours, people had been out searching for Rosie. Drones had gone up and tracked the area. Nothing was successful. However, once we went back to the bus stop, Sabat had found her within 25 minutes. It was amazing.

For the past few years, he has been my hero dog. He's broken me out of my pain, lifted me from my deep sadness and made me laugh on countless occasions. Is he spoilt? Of course he is, but he deserves it too. When you fall in love with a significant other, you think you know love and you do, on a human level. But all dog owners know this too. The love you receive from a dog is different. It's pure and it makes your life better. That alone is worthy of keeping a dog, 'til death you do part.

Chapter 24
Deja vu

As I pull into the car park, I'm surprised by how busy it is. The last time I was here, there were just a few cars and not many people either. Now the place is heaving. It's four years and four months since I was last in this place. Kirsty and I were planning to return in 2022. After her passing there were a couple of other times I had planned to make the journey, but on a whim, I had decided to make the trip yesterday. The date is 29th August 2025 and it's just after 2pm. I am back at Gretna Green where we were married on 30th April 2021.

It's windy, but quite warm as I walk across the car park and through the archway that proclaims 'Gretna Green – since 1754.'

It seems that most people are tourists, intrigued by the romance and stories of this place. There are wedding photos being taken in the square under the massive interlocking hands. At that moment I feel the emotion build in my chest and feel the tears well up in me. I hadn't expected this much emotion and for a moment, it catches me by surprise. My memory shows me a picture of Kirsty smiling, wearing jeans, a jacket and a blue t-shirt holding up her hand and proudly showing her wedding ring. That was a day of complete joy. Shortly after that we set off on our honeymoon around Cumbria, stopping first at Hadrian's Wall. Today, the emptiness of the place fills my heart. I stop and compose myself.

Under my arm is my wedding album. I pull it tighter towards me and head a for a sign that says 'Entry'.

I enter a building that has changed beyond recognition since I was last here. In fact, it has changed so much I can't even remember what was here before. What is here now is a gift shop (Walt Disney would be proud of how many there are). Directly in front of me is a reception desk and to my left the entrance to the Famous Old Blacksmith's Shop museum tour. The lady manning the reception was busy with customers, so I wandered around the shop.

At this point, it might be useful to explain why Gretna Green is the romance capital of the world. In other words, not the Elvis chapel in Las Vegas.

The first marriage vows, as couples speak them today, were written in 1549 by Thomas Cranmer, the Archbishop of Canterbury. Various changes were made until Hardwicke's Marriage Act came into being on 25th March 1754. However, this related only to England and not all of the UK. What was important about this Act was that it prevented young people, under the age of 21, from marrying without parental control.

At the time, Gretna Green, being only one mile inside the Scottish border, was a place where you could still be legally married without those restrictions. As it was on the main route to Glasgow and horses and carriages were the main form of transport at the time, a blacksmith was in demand. The blacksmith was also seen as an upstanding citizen and as such could perform weddings. These became known as 'anvil priests'. The first of these was Joseph Paisley who married thousands of couples in his tenure.

Rules and laws have changed over the years, but the romance of Gretna Green has endured and now it is the centre of romance in the UK and its reputation is known around the world. The day I was there, there were fourteen weddings at the

Blacksmith's Shop and another six at the Gretna Hall Hotel. There may have been more spread across the town.

Should you ever wish to get married there, and I do highly recommend it, make sure of two things. One, that you marry at Gretna Green and not Gretna, the slightly larger town a mile away and two, you marry in the original room at the Famous Old Blacksmith's Shop. That's the one with the anvil on the plinth and has raised steps where guests watch the couple getting married.

Back to the present day.

The lady comes back to the reception desk. The shop has gone quiet for a moment and I tell her my story. That we were married here a few days after Covid restrictions were lifted, that all the guests wore masks, but the bride and groom couldn't get Covid on our wedding day, so we were exempt (!). The lady's name was Helen and she told me that she had begun work there in August 2021, a few months after our wedding. She listened politely and then I dropped the bombshell. When she heard that Kirsty had died, she took a sharp intake of breath. I asked if she'd liked to see our wedding album. It consists of the twelve best photos from the day and they are beautifully produced. She said she would and as I turned to the photos of Kirsty and me, she said how beautiful she was. I agreed. When I told her that Kirsty was only 41 when she died her shock deepened. All of this was hard to share, but this stranger had become my new friend.

We talked a little more and I bought a ticket to the exhibition. She explained that I couldn't see the actual wedding room until later in the day as weddings were going on as we spoke.

'The room is free after 4pm,' she said.

'So, I can come back at four and I'll be able to see it?' I asked.

‘Yes,’ she said and smiled.

‘Thank you,’ I said, then I paused. ‘Guess what time we got married?’

‘Four o’clock?’ she said.

‘Yes.’

‘Oh my god, I’ve got chills,’ and she shivered.

So here I was. Four years and four months after we were married, I would be back in the wedding room at the same time, on a Friday, the same day at the end of the month. When I got home, I realised that the time I stayed in Carnforth and Gretna Green totalled four hours and forty minutes and the drive from Gretna Green back to Simon’s to pick up Sabat was four hours and forty minutes as well. Coincidence is coincidence and strange happenings are difficult to explain.

A couple of weeks after this, I was telling my hairdresser, Kelly, this story. She said, ‘You know three 4’s is an Angel number, don’t you?’ I replied that I’d never heard of Angel Numbers. Kelly told me to repeat the story to the salon owner, Vickie. When I’d finished, Vickie said she has goosebumps all over and explained ‘Angel numbers’ to me.

There are angel numbers, but repeating number 444 is the number code of the angelic realm. The angels are connecting with you whenever you see this number. Literally, when you see this number, know that your angels are nearby. Even more so than other angel numbers! If you’ve been wondering if your prayers or intentions are being heard, this is a big green flag. Manifestation is in progress!

Until that day, I’d never heard of angel numbers, but the coincidences continue to stack up and they are always in my favour. Like a guardian angel is looking after me. Believe what you will. I just observe what happens.

I had taken the wedding album on a whim, that perhaps it would be easier to show the pictures than share the story in too much depth. It definitely made it all seem real. After Kirsty died, I had bought a small, blue teardrop urn that I filled with her ashes. I had brought that with me too, but that stayed in the car. Nevertheless, it was hard not to think that some of her was with me.

I walked through the exhibition and saw the original anvil from 1754 (too brittle to use now, the one in use these days dates back to 1940) and it is a nice trip through history. I strolled around the shops complex and bought biscuits and Tunnock's tea cakes and sheltered from a rain shower in the café that was the Wee Big Shop when I was there in 2021. 4 o'clock arrived and I went back to the exhibition.

Helen took me through and there it was. The wedding room, now empty, exactly as it was four years before and exactly as it had been when Joseph Paisley married those first English runaways 271 years earlier. A few people came through and walked about and then it was just me in the room again. Me and the anvil. No one else. I could see Kirsty standing at the entrance, her arm in her father's and her sister just behind her. On the steps behind me were Noah, Caroline and her daughter, Gabbie. Noah's partner, Akeem was resplendent in a blue suit and Kirsty's family were on the steps behind my left shoulder. I could see it all.

I took my photos and I let my memories wash over me. I was okay now. All I felt was love and happiness. This was where my favourite day had been. There was no hint of all I would go through a year later. This would always be a happy place, a peaceful place, a beautiful place. So many people get married there every year and yet, to me, it felt mine.

I left the room and saw the rest of the exhibition and retraced my steps, seeing the way in and following it around. Helen reappeared and talked me through some of the changes that had happened in the time since 2021 and then it was time to leave. Mission accomplished. Emotions intact.

The Gretna Hall Hotel is a one-minute drive away, so I went there as well. Another wedding was taking place, behind closed doors, so I took some more photos in the grounds and went into the hotel. Again, I shared my story; again the reception staff were shocked at the sadness and they let me take a look around. I could see the reception room we had booked and from the outside, saw the room that we stayed in. Now it was time to go home.

My journey home was easy, the A1 chosen, the M6 ignored. It was a good choice. Sabat was excited to see me, but had clearly loved spending time with Simon and Ash, the Collie, all day.

After a good sleep and a Saturday morning lie-in Sabat and I began the day with a trip to the bakers, then into the village to the butchers. I tied Sabat by his lead to a lamppost directly outside. When the butcher's wife saw him, she followed me out with two bags of meat treats. I thanked her and we headed to some local woods for a walk.

Sabat did what he does. Sniffs everything, pees everywhere and did his business. I did what I do. I bagged the poo, spoke to other dog owners and reflected on the previous day.

The circle felt complete. It's me and the dog and in the future, someone will share this life with us. Kirsty and I were together for 626 days. However long my life will be, they will always be tremendously important days, but I will continue to live and make a new life. That is the only way past grief. Love never dies; that's my belief, but new love can be found.

I also realised that the way we feel about celebrities that die and those we know is different. Almost fifty years after he died, Elvis seems as alive as ever. New films, new music and articles and books still being written about him. The same is true for Marilyn Monroe, James Dean and other icons of the past. Imagine now talking about your loved ones in this way. Their memory will never fade. Their presence will always be felt and that's the way I treat those who have left this spinning globe.

The love that Sabat and I have is another bond that will never be broken and he has taught me how to live, how to cope and taught me a new purpose. Who knows? One day I might even be able to write Dog Walking for the Advanced. Thanks for staying with me this far. Keep walking ...

Epilogue
Owls

My mum loved owls. All sorts of owls. She had various stuffed ones around the house. She was quite the animal lover. In her time, she had rabbits and guinea pigs, but eventually she stopped keeping them.

But she never had an owl. She just loved them.

I began writing this book in March 2025, but writing about Kirsty's passing and events around that time led to me leaving it for a while. The bulk of the work was done in the summer and autumn of 2025. When I started writing, my mother seemed in good health, but from May onwards she had one health issue after another.

She was born Diana Jacqueline on 17th June 1938. Kirsty's birthday was 14th June 1980, so the only occasion they ever met was at a birthday party for both of them at my parent's house. Mum approved highly of Kirsty.

When Kirsty died, everyone got together to support me. It helped massively.

In August 2025, I was surprised to get a WhatsApp from mum to say that they had moved house to Lincolnshire. They had bought a beautiful bungalow nestled in two acres of land. I was even more shocked when mum was rushed into hospital in Boston, ten days later. She had fractured her back and developed similar stomach issues to ones she had had before. Later tests showed that she had gall bladder cancer.

She was moved into a care home and she passed away on Monday 20th October 2025, just a week before this book went to print.

By good fortune, I visited her that Monday morning. Dad was with her, as he had been for all the time she was being treated. I had taken a galley (draft) copy of this book with me, as I wanted to show mum the photo of her in it. She was quite weak by then, but she smiled when she saw the photo of her and Sabat. Dad left and would return later which left me alone with mum for the best part of half-an-hour.

I gave her water when she asked for it, held her hand to keep her warm and told her I loved her. I also asked her to send me a sign when she had gone. I wasn't sure how long that would be and I wasn't sure if I should have asked it, but I did. I said goodbye and was doubtful I would see her on the Wednesday. However, I spoke to a nurse who assured me that mum wasn't weak and I would see her then.

I later learned that ten minutes after I left mum's organs began to shut down. She had decided that enough was enough. She passed away about two hours later with Dad at her side. He sent me a text to let me know, but I didn't see that and had it confirmed by my sister just after 5pm. I was shocked. I hadn't expected the end to come so quickly.

But also, when I heard the news Sabat and I had just returned from a dog walk. On that walk, one of four regular routes that we take, I had seen a small wooden owl on a fence. I was surprised to say the least. It had never been there before and I thought it couldn't be a sign as mum was still alive. What I didn't know what that she had passed about an hour before.

Before Kirsty died I always thought that once you were dead, that was it. No more. Over the past three-and-a-half years, I have seen and experienced many things that have given me a double take.

People will fall into three categories: one, those who think that you die and that's it. Two, people who are agnostic and three, people who believe in all the signs. Whichever works for you, that's great by me. I'm in camp two. I guess we only really know when we learn for ourselves.

I now feel incredibly grateful for that Monday morning and because of the awful grief I went through with Kirsty, I can manage the emotion in a more composed way.

Mum had 87 years and I was lucky to have her as my mother. Kirsty only had 41 years and I was lucky to have her as my wife. I will miss both of them for the rest of my days, as you will with anyone you have lost. If you are someone who is helping a person with their last days, I hope this book has helped you in some small way, in the same way that I trust it has helped those who know the pain of bereavement.

Thank you for being part of my journey too. If you need further help, than I heartily recommend you get a dog. They are the most wonderful companions. There is also further help in the Appendices.

Everything you need is at the end of a lead.

Appendix 1:
A Promise To Felix

A Promise to Felix Dog Rescue started as an idea to help a little pup called Felix come over to the UK from Romania and find him a lovely forever home. The dogs in Romania and other countries are often treated as vermin. They are tortured, abused and thrown out onto the streets as trash. They are rounded up and sent to the kill shelter to die a terrible death. Laura saves as many as she can from there and takes them to her shelter. We have sponsored and still sponsor dogs at Laura's shelter.

We have bought dogs over since 2018 and have saved and found forever homes for thousands. This came from an idea for one little dog but has become so much more and with wonderful supporters, donations and adopters. This is a group that are passionate about helping these dogs in need and although still very small in comparison to other rescue groups, can only go from strength to strength with your support.

Sadly, we have stopped bringing dogs over for the time being as it's increasingly harder to get dogs adopted in the UK. We still support Laura by sponsoring dogs in her shelter and we have forever foster dogs in our care still.

Michele Scott.

Website: www.apromisetofelix.co.uk

Appendix 2:
Top Tens
For Beginners

For walking:

1. On the lead – most of the time.
2. Off lead – in the wild fields or when other dogs want to play.
3. Always seek permission to play.
4. If your dog approaches another dog apologise or be polite (whichever is appropriate).
5. When walking your dog with others, don't be a dick.
6. Keep to a routine.
7. Get out every day.
8. Teach them road safety fundamentals.
9. Vary the routes.
10. Get a light collar for the dark nights and early mornings.

For running:

1. Accept that running with a dog takes patience.
2. Have a good harness that fits around your middle and doesn't fall off.
3. Build the miles up. All dogs are different and can cope with different mileage. Only run with huskies if you love running over 10 miles every time.
4. Poo bags are just as essential as they are when walking.
5. Get used to stopping (for sniffing or peeing), but you control the run, not the dog.
6. Avoid busy walking times unless you want your run compromised.
7. Keep your dog away from the traffic. A rabbit could kill you and your dog.
8. Have fun; don't get frustrated.
9. Start slowly, even though your dog may want to run you down the road. Dogs get even more excited running than they do walking.
10. All dogs can run. I've seen Shih Tzus running, but carrying a Shih Tzu home is different to carrying a Great Dane. Know your dog. If you have a Shepherd, Collie or Husky, then they might carry you home.

Keeping you and your dog happy

1. Make your dog feel loved.
2. Regular exercise keeps them alert.
3. Establish the rules. Most dogs get spoiled, but don't overdo it.
4. It's ok to sleep on the sofa. And on the bed. Not in the bed!
5. Find them a pack. Most dogs love being around other dogs.
6. Try not to leave them more than six hours at a time.
7. Find a great dogsitter. It will give you freedom in your life.
8. Walk them before bedtime. It saves on accidents and makes it more comfortable for the dog.
9. Play with them daily. It keeps their mind stimulated.
10. A dog's life is reflected in the experiences you give them.

Before tragedy strikes:

1. Plan your funeral (or celebration of life) in advance.
2. Do it together (no matter your age).
3. Talk to your children about it. Act like an adult. By planning for death, you get to live your life.
4. Burial or cremation?
5. Religious or otherwise?
6. Choose the music. You get up to five pieces you can choose.
7. Decide the dress code. Formal or informal, black or colours?
8. Record a video of each other so you can hear their voice after they've gone.
9. Take lots of photos and file them sensibly.
10. Record your passwords and PIN numbers for phones, laptops, PCs, streaming services and bank accounts. Put them in a book and put the book in a fireproof box or safe. You will also need your National Insurance number, passport and driver's licence.

Lessons from this book:

1. Love never dies.
2. Love can be found again.
3. Record their voice.
4. Take lots of photos and video.
5. Plan your funeral.
6. Make a will.
7. Let unexplained things happen. Believe whatever you believe.
8. Keep making progress.
9. Humour helps everything.
10. Dogs make everything easier.

About the author:

A public speaker, a writer, a publisher, a martial artist and a dog owner. Not necessarily in that order. Andy lives with Sabat and can be found wandering the footpaths of the East Midlands, usually muttering to himself. Sabat sniffs in appreciation.
'Dog Walking For Beginners' is his sixth book.

Others can be found on his website:
www.andygibney.com or on Amazon.
More information about the stories in this book can be found at www.dogwalkingforbeginners.co.uk

Other titles:
The Magic Number
How to Seduce your Wife
Punching Above My Height
Top of the Pile
A Dash Between Two Dates